WROXETER

Life & Death of a Roman City

Roger White & Philip Barker

TEMPUS

VIROCONIUM

Virocon – Virocon –
Still the ancient name rings on
And brings, in the untrampled wheat,
The tumult of a thousand feet.

Where trumpets rang and men marched by,
None passes but the dragon-fly,
Athwart the grassy town, forlorn,
The lone dor-beetle blows his horn.

The poppy standards droop and fall
Above one rent and mournful wall:
In every sunset-flame it burns,
Yet towers unscathed when day returns.

And still the breaking seas of grain
Flow havenless across the plain:
The years wash on, their spindrift leaps
Where the old city, dreaming, sleeps.

Grief lingers here, like mists that lie
Across the dawns of ripe July;
On capital and corridor
The pathos of the conqueror.

The pillars stand with alien grace,
In churches of a younger race;
The chiselled column, black and rough,
Becomes a roadside cattle-trough:

The skulls of men who, right or wrong,
Still wore the splendour of the strong,
Are shepherds' lanterns now, and shield
Their candles in the lambing field.

But when through evening's open door,
Two lovers tread the broken floor,
And the wild-apple petals fall
Round passion's scarlet festival;

When cuckoos call from the green gloom
Where dark shelving forests loom;
When foxes bark beside the gate,
And the grey badger seeks his mate –

There haunts within them secretly
One that lives while empires die,
A shrineless god whose songs abide
Forever in the countryside.

Mary Webb

First published 1998
Reprinted 1999
Revised edition 2002

PUBLISHED IN THE UNITED KINGDOM BY:
Tempus Publishing Ltd
The Mill, Brimscombe Port
Stroud, Gloucestershire GL5 2QG

PUBLISHED IN THE UNITED STATES OF AMERICA BY:
Tempus Publishing Inc.
2A Cumberland Street
Charleston, SC 29401

Tempus books are available in France and Germany
from the following addresses:

Tempus Publishing Group
21 Avenue de la République
37300 Joué-lès-Tours
FRANCE

Tempus Publishing Group
Gustav-Adolf-Straße 3
99084 Erfurt
GERMANY

British Library Cataloguing in Publication Data.
A catalogue record for this book is available from the British Library.

ISBN 0 7524 1409 7

Typesetting and origination by Tempus Publishing.
PRINTED AND BOUND IN GREAT BRITAIN.

Contents

List of illustrations and acknowledgements

The authors are extremely grateful to a number of institutions and individuals for agreeing to supply illustrations for this book, all of whom retain copyright to their images (figures or colour plates credited in brackets): Aerofilms Ltd (**9**); Birmingham and Warwickshire Archaeological Society (**30**); British Telecom & BUFAU (**colour plate 14**); BUFAU (**31**; **colour plate 5**); Clwyd-Powys Archaeological Trust (**14, 29**; **colour plate 22**); Cambridge University Commitee for Aerial Photography (**20, 72**); English Heritage (**8, 10, 17, 25, 53, 55-6, 58-65, 67**; **colour plates 6-9, 17, 20, 21, 23, 24**); English Heritage Ancient Monuments Laboratory and Geographical Surveys of Bradford (**colour plate 3**); the Trustees of the Haverfield Bequest (**22, 40**); *Illustrated London News* picture library (**45**); Royal Commission for Historical Monuments of England (**32, 33, 69**); Rowley's House Museum, Shrewsbury (**24, 47, 50**; **colour plates 4, 11, 18**); Shropshire Records and Research Centre (**3, 4, 6**; **colour plate 2**); Society of Antiquaries of London (**49**); Sotheby's (**colour plate 1**); and the University of Birmingham special collections (**2, 70, 74**). The individuals comprise: Dr Arnold Baker (**11, 21**); Steve Cosh (**colour plate 15**); Donald Mackreth (**36, 44, 46**); Dr David Neal (**colour plate 16**); Prof. Nishimura and Dr Dean Goodman (**37**); and Dr Graham Webster (**19, 43, *52***).

Permission to reprint Mary Webb's poem was kindly granted by Timothy Cape. All the remaining illustrations were drawn by the authors or were taken from photographs by them, although permission to reproduce one of the author's photographs of the Trier ceiling panels (**colour plate 19**) was kindly granted by the Bischöfliches Dom- und Diözesanmuseum, Trier. Especial thanks are due to Graham Norrie of the Department of Ancient History and Archaeology at the University of Birmingham who prepared the photographic plates from line drawings and slides, and to Paul Davies of Rowley's House museum for taking **colour plate 4**.

Text figures

Colour plates (between pages 64 and 65)

The *cover illustration* shows the western baths suite, in front of the Old Work, with the Wrekin in the background

Preface

Both authors have lived with Wroxeter for a long time. Our association comes from our work together on the baths basilica site where one of us (PAB) was site director from 1966, and the other (RHW) was first a member of the digging staff and then ultimately a supervisor. From 1987, the junior partner of this team was coordinating the writing up of the baths basilica site, based in the cottage above the forum within the Roman city. From there, with an unparalleled view of the Old Work and Wrekin through the window, much time was spent in working on the archaeology of the baths basilica and the city. When this task was completed, in 1994, the collaborative effort continued through the work on the city's surroundings through the Wroxeter Hinterland Project. The present book thus rests on long consideration of the archaeology of the city and its surroundings by both of us, but could never have been possible without the work and thoughts of our many collaborators and colleagues throughout the years. Specifically, we should like to thank the other members of the baths basilica post-excavation team, Dr Kate Pretty, Mike Corbishley and Heather Bird whose stimulating and rigorous debates on the nature and meaning of the evidence did so much to focus the final publication of the excavation.

We should also like to thank those working at Wroxeter at the same time as us, not least Dr Graham Webster who has done so much to elucidate Wroxeter's development – and Donald Mackreth whose rigorous approach to the complex structural remains of the baths in particular has clarified much of its history. Arnold Baker and David Pannett both generously provided valuable insights into aspects of Wroxeter through their respective fields of aerial archaeology and the study of the River Severn. Bruce Bennison and Mike Stokes, the past and present curators of archaeology at Rowley's House Museum, Shrewsbury, have considerably aided our work by making accessible the important collections they supervise, whilst Mike Watson, county archaeologist in Shropshire, has provided much useful and thoughtful criticism and ideas over the years.

None of what has been achieved at Wroxeter in the last 40 years would have been possible without the enlightened encouragement of English Heritage and, before them, the Ministry of Public Buildings and Works and the Department of the Environment. The long-term nature of the excavations, and the many branches of the organisation, mean that so many individuals have been involved in that period that it is not possible to list them by name here. Nonetheless, our gratitude for their help is no less sincere for that. The work of the Wroxeter Hinterland Project, which developed out of the excavations at Wroxeter, was made possible by a grant from the Leverhulme Trust. Further generous financial support for aspects of the project was received from the Roman Research Trust, The Society for the Promotion of Roman Studies, The PC Ellerman foundation, The Margaret Guido Trust, Geoscan Research, The Mercer's Company of London, The Walker Trust, The Yapp Trust, The Mary Webb Trust, Barclay's Bank plc, The Roger and Sarah Bancroft Clark Trust, and The C.B. and H.H.

Taylor Trust. The virtual reality reconstruction of Wroxeter, which aims to give a three-dimensional picture of the city throughout its life and will be used as part of an interactive educational package, was created as part of a project funded by a British Telecom University Development Award. Details will be found in the further reading section at the end of this book.

Our colleagues at Birmingham University, and in particular Simon Buteux, Peter Ellis, Jane Evans, Sally Exon, Vince Gaffney and Martijn van Leusen, deserve a special mention for their comments on earlier drafts. We are also extremely grateful to our colleagues in the Ancient Monuments Laboratory and Geophysical Surveys of Bradford who carried out the bulk of the geophysical work to such exemplary standards. Jon Guite and the volunteers on the Wroxeter Hinterland Project too deserve special mention for their sterling work in the thankless task of carrying out the resistivity survey of Wroxeter, and for fieldwalking in Wroxeter's hinterland.

We should also like to thank Peter Kemmis Betty for commissioning the book in the first place, and Guy de la Bédoyère for his stringent editorial criticisms which have done so much to improve the text. Responsibility for any faults that remain, however, must rest with us.

This work attempts to bridge that uncomfortable gap between being of interest to the general reader whilst supplying useful information to colleagues working in the field. For the latter, there may not be enough detail, whilst for the former there may be too much. We would ask our colleagues to be patient a little longer. The evidence behind what must sometimes seem like guesswork rests on mostly unpublished research which will appear in print in the not too-distant future. For those whose interest is more general, we hope that this work will satisfy their curiosity about the site, although avenues for further reading are suggested in a short list at the end of the book.

And last, we must pay tribute to the support we have received from our wives. Eve and Fran have also lived with Wroxeter for a very long time: we would like to dedicate this book to them.

Preface to revised edition

During the last year of Philip's life, he and I reworked chapter 7, the story of the Dark Age town, at his instigation. We managed to finalise it before he died in January 2001. What had caught his eye was the recent thinking about the possible causes of the so-called '540 Event' which is evidenced in tree-ring chronologies throughout the world. While we still do not know exactly what caused this catastrophic climatic event, he was struck by the coincidence that it had occurred at the same time as the major changes seen at Wroxeter – the Great Rebuilding – and wished at least to suggest a possible link between that radical change in the town's appearance and this dramatic natural event. I tell this story partly to demonstrate that even while gravely ill, Philip's mind was still as sharp as ever, and to show that he was never satisfied that he had completed his work at Wroxeter.

His passing was a great blow to all who knew him, but especially to those who worked closely with him. I for one will miss his trenchant, but constructive, criticism, and his ability to add grace, eloquence and clarity to my writing. Archaeology's loss was, however, even greater.

Roger White, May 2002

Introduction

Wroxeter Roman City is one of Britain's more neglected archaeological sites, a surprising fact given that it was the fourth largest town in Roman Britain and must hold an untold wealth of information on life in one of Rome's more distant provinces. The site lies in the heart of England, in sight of the Welsh border and surrounded by the spectacular scenery of the Welsh Marches. It sits perched on the east bank of the River Severn, overlooking its floodplain extending towards the Welsh hills and within sight of the medieval town of Shrewsbury. To the east, the view is dominated by the hump-backed hill known as the Wrekin whose massive presence seems to brood over the landscape and probably gave the Roman city its name *Viroconium Cornoviorum,* that is, 'The settlement of Virico of the *Cornovii* tribe'. Behind the Wrekin lies the New Town of Telford, a modern-day counterpart to the Roman city. It too was founded as a result of government initiative and like its predecessor has had an enormous impact on its surroundings. Throughout the 1970s, while we were excavating at Wroxeter, we were always highly amused by a sign in an otherwise barren wasteland proclaiming 'Telford Town Centre', still to be built. And yet the picture at Wroxeter in about 120, when the Emperor Hadrian may have visited the new city, must have been very similar: unfinished public buildings, newly-built houses, and everywhere the bustle of city life. Telford has only begun to run its course whilst at Wroxeter we can see the whole span of its life from foundation to desertion (**1**).

This book, the first about Wroxeter Roman City for 125 years, aims to tell the story of the way in which the city was established after a brief period of army occupation, how it flourished within the Roman Empire, and how it outlasted the Western Roman Empire by 150 years. The story will be viewed through the lens of archaeology, a lens that can provide an immediacy to the account that cannot be found in the dry historical texts of the day written in far-away Rome or Constantinople. But the same lens also limits the possible view. It can tell us the conditions under which people lived but less about their thoughts or beliefs.

The following chapters outline the story of the excavation of Wroxeter and then the story of the city itself beginning with the legionary fortress and its soldiers, some of whom we know from their tombstones or discharge certificates. Their names hint at the exotic nature of the people of the Empire, of the possibility of natives of Syria or North Africa coming to our colder climes to live and work among the people of Britain. For

1 *Stages in the rise and fall of Wroxeter Roman city. Top left: the fortress (c.57–90); top right: the early city (c.90–150); bottom left: the mature city (c.150–500); bottom right: the sub-Roman town (c.500–650)*

the most part, however, they seem to be from the neighbourhood of Gaul or Thrace, Europeans who may well have spoken a form of Celtic that the locals understood. The impact of the Roman army on the local population is also considered. Even though the tribe may have been aware of the conquest of Britain by Rome, the arrival of the army must have been a profound shock, exacerbated by the seizure of land to build numerous campaign and garrison forts. Overnight, the locals will have had to get used to concepts such as money rather than barter and will have been overwhelmed by the range and quantity of imported goods arriving in the area. Nonetheless, the population seems to have adjusted readily to the change and swiftly adopted the Roman life style so that, within two generations of the Romans' arrival in the area, the new town was flourishing, its public buildings under construction and impressive town houses already inhabited.

Much of the story of the development of the city and its private buildings is yet to be discovered since such a small proportion of the site has been excavated but glimpses of the life of its citizens have been seen through small-scale excavations of houses and the larger-scale excavations of its public buildings. We know that they had a wide choice of goods in the city's markets, that they worshipped gods both in their homes and in public temples, and that they enjoyed visits to the impressive bath house provided for them. Life seems to have continued without a great deal of change for several centuries but gradually the people and their pattern of life altered, in parallel with developments in the wider Empire. The adoption of Christianity, the increasingly tenuous links with central government, and the imposition of direct rule over a once self-governing community are the more obvious signs of change in the later Empire but it is not clear how much these registered with or affected Wroxeter's citizens. All we can say is that the demise of Roman rule in Britain, early in the fifth century, appears to have had little discernible impact on the city and its inhabitants. They seem to have continued much as before until the very end of that century when, in a spectacular renaissance, the whole city centre was reorganised. At the centre of this reorganisation, on the site of the baths basilica, was a mansion nearly 120 Roman feet (35.5m) long and over 50 Roman feet (14.5m) in width surrounded by smaller ancillary buildings. We shall never know for certain who lived in this house, be it one of the 'tyrants', described by the sixth-century monk Gildas, or Wroxeter's bishop, but whoever it was ensured that some form of town life continued for Wroxeter's citizens until a new power, the Anglo-Saxon kingdom of Mercia, took over the area in the seventh century. This sounded the death-knell for the city; a misfortune for its inhabitants but a blessing for us since it has meant that Wroxeter, largely unoccupied from that date, has come down to us through the centuries to offer us a glimpse into the long-vanished but seemingly familiar world of Rome.

1 The rediscovery of Wroxeter

The 'Old Work', the largest fragment of a Roman civilian building still standing in Britain, has been an isolated landmark in Shropshire's landscape for many centuries, emerging as the rest of the Roman city was robbed of its stone and timber, or disintegrated back into the earth. It must have excited wonder in all who saw it, especially during the centuries up to the Norman Conquest, when most major buildings were of wood, and when even stone-built churches were dwarfed by the scale of Roman fragments, 'the work of Giants', as the writer of the Anglo-Saxon poem *The Ruin* puts it.

Despite the fame of the Old Work, antiquarian interest in Wroxeter was surprisingly slow to develop, which can perhaps be attributed to the site's remoteness. Despite this, there is strong evidence that for local people the ruins were a source of endless stories and myths, some recorded by Thomas Wright, the first antiquarian to excavate at the site. The most notable, the *History of Fulk Fitz Warine*, records that when William I had conquered the area he camped by the burnt and buried ruins of a very large town. A local Briton told him that the site was called Castle Bran. It had been built by Brutus, Corineus, and other knights, all descended from Troy. They had conquered the land by defeating the giants who lived there, the greatest being Geomagog who was only killed after mortal combat with Corineus. Geomagog's spirit had haunted the land and driven the Britons out of the town. Long after, Bran, son of King Donwal, rebuilt the town, but the devil came in the night and took away everything since which time no-one had lived there again. On hearing this, King William's champion, Payn Peveril, and fifteen other knights vowed to stay in the ruins overnight to fight Geomagog. The giant's spirit was overcome by the Cross carried by Peveril and related where the knight might find a great treasure put in a house he had made underground.

Such stories undoubtedly drove the activities of the locals in the quest for buried treasure, as can be seen from the records of the Court of King's Bench for 1292 which details an early instance of a breach of the Treasure Trove law, formulated originally by King John to protect the Crown's right to bullion found by accident or by design. The four accused, William son of William of Hodeney (Hodnet), Walter de [Market] Drayton, William Parson of Ledewych, and Richard Tyffe, had 'dug by night at Wroccestre, in search of treasure'. Only the latter two appeared in court since the first named was already in prison while the second had died. The charges were dismissed as 'though they had dug as aforesaid, they had found nothing'. Presumably other such

2 *A drawing of 'The Old work of Wroxeter in Shropshire' in 1721*

instances and more casual discoveries continued to be made although there are no further records of them.

The first antiquarian account of Wroxeter is that from William Camden, Clarenceux King of Arms in the Court of Heralds to Queen Elizabeth I, who compiled a descriptive account of all the antiquities of Britain called *Britannia* (1586). His account is brief. After noting that the site was the ancient '*Uriconium;* for so Antoninus called it' (i.e. the *Antonine Itinerary*, see chapter 6), he continues 'Here is nothing to be seen of it, but a very few reliques of broken walls, call'd by the people *The old works of Wroxeter*, which were built of hewn stone, and laid in seven rows, arch'd within after the fashion of the Britains (*sic*)'. A note adds that this fragment stands 'in the centre of the city, being about 20 foot high, and 100 in length', dimensions which accord well with the present state of the Old Work and with the first known illustration of the monument, a schematised version dated to the 1720s (**2**). This may be contrasted with the more accurate rendition published in the *Gentleman's Magazine* in 1812 (**3**). Thus, the Old Work must have become a ruin well before the beginning of the sixteenth century. Camden's account goes on: 'That where these [walls] are, was formerly a castle, is probable from the unevenness of the ground, heaps of earth, and here and there the rubbish of walls. The plot where this city stood (which is no small spot of ground) is a blacker earth than the rest [of the area], and yields the largest crops of best barley.' Camden's book was updated in 1695 by Gough who added a substantial amount of additional material derived from the records of the Society of Antiquaries of London. In particular, he describes the remains of the city defences as being 'built upon a foundation for the most part made of pebble-stones; about 3 yards thick, and a vast trench round it, which in some places appears exceeding deep to this day.' He also noted the occurrence of many coins on the site 'some whereof are of gold, tho' but rarely found; ...& others of silver,

3 *An engraving of 'The Roman Wall at Wroxeter', 1812 by D. Parkes*

very commonly met with; and the rest of brass, copper, and mixed metals. They are called by the inhabitants *Dynders'*, a word which he surmised derived from the Latin word *denarius*. Gough noted that all these coins were, without exception, Roman in date and thus proved that the city had not been taken over by the Anglo-Saxons.

Sadly, Gough's updated edition was too early for the first archaeologically-recorded building from Wroxeter which was found in 1701. Its discovery is of interest for the proof it affords of how aware the locals were of what lay beneath the fields. The account tells us that a Mr Clayton, wishing to obtain building stone, went to a part of a field where he knew that stone lay close to the surface as he had seen marks on the ground in hot weather caused by plants parching in the shallow soils above buried walls. When he dug there, he hit upon a hypocausted building which was recorded by John Lyster, a local antiquarian who communicated the results of the excavation to the Royal Philosophical Society of London, along with a clearly inaccurate and schematised plan of the building. Far more accurately recorded was the building excavated by the young Thomas Telford in 1788 while he was working on the new Shrewsbury to Ironbridge road, now the modern B4380, whose route cuts diagonally across Wroxeter between the sites of the north-west and south-east gates. Telford had no great respect for antiquities when it came to road building: this same road smashed through the cloister of Shrewsbury's Abbey, isolating its refectory pulpit from the rest of the building with an insensitivity that road builders and developers have been emulating ever since. His attitude to the building at Wroxeter, however, seems to have been quite different. One can only surmise that his precise architectural drawings, including a plan and an isometric (perspective) view, indicate the enormous interest that the budding engineer took in the technical skill of Roman architects (**4**).

At about the same time as Telford was working at Wroxeter, antiquarians began to take notice of the many casual finds found on Wroxeter's fields and report them to the Society

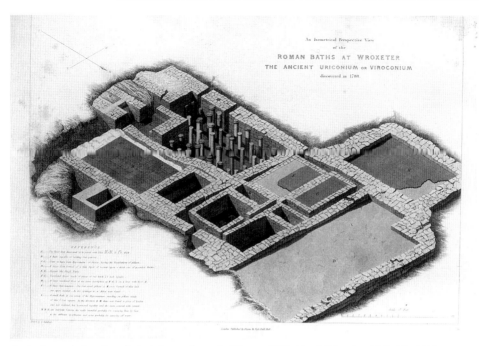

4 *An isometric drawing of a bath house, drawn by Thomas Telford in 1788 and published in 1838*

of Antiquaries of London or to the *Gentleman's Magazine*. Among these early finds are an eye-doctor's medicine stamp still extant at Rowley's House Museum, Shrewsbury, and the three complete tombstones which were all found in the cemetery area east of the city (see **22**). Finds of statuettes in bronze, stonework, or of coins and other artefacts get equal prominence in the record showing the eclectic tastes of the gentlemen scholars of the day. Wroxeter fitted in too with the Romantic movement, its picturesque ruined wall providing an ideal foil for the watercolourist's eye. Even such an eminent artist as Thomas Girtin took care to make his record of the Old Work, although comparison with a contemporary watercolour painted by Revd. Williams, the Vicar of Battlefield Church, Shrewsbury, shows that Girtin felt free to alter and romanticise his subject by adding a pond and a few shrubs to his view of the north side of the Old Work, in contrast to the ploughed field that Williams shows. The recent excavations have shown that Williams' version was the more accurate (**colour plates 1 & 2**).

Casual records and discoveries continued to be made throughout the eighteenth and into the nineteenth century and gradually accounts of the archaeology of the area were drawn together, notably by Thomas Farmer Dukes whose work survives in a manuscript dated to 1829 in the library of the Society of Antiquaries of London. Only an abridged version of this manuscript was ever published, and then merely as a contribution to a congress of the British Archaeological Association, but the manuscript does preserve some interesting information, not least illustrations of the known mosaics of Wroxeter and the area. These have to be used with care, however, as a comparison between his reconstruction of the mosaic found at Wroxeter in 1827 with that shown here (**colour plate 15**), shows that Dukes had little understanding of how to restore mosaic

15

5 *A portrait of Thomas Wright, taken in the 1860s*

pavements on paper. The mosaic itself, incidentally, was destroyed by sightseers from Shrewsbury, in an early example of souvenir hunting. Two other mosaics he published had been found in 1706 and 1734. Neither appears to be an accurate record, although that found in 1706 bears a resemblance to the mosaic found at Whitley Grange (**colour plate 16**), whilst the other is a fragment thought to be from a fourth-century design.

As Duke's description of Shropshire was never fully published, Hartshorne's *Salopia Antiqua*, published in 1841, must be counted as the first serious assessment of the archaeology of the county, including Wroxeter. These syntheses were in themselves valuable but added little knowledge and it was not until the next generation of antiquaries took an interest in Wroxeter that a real understanding of the monument began to develop. This new generation, epitomised by men like the London chemist Charles Roach Smith who, virtually single-handed, rescued London's archaeology from Victorian redevelopers, took archaeology and ancient history from the arcane and limited world in which it had been founded into the public domain. The work of archaeologists in Europe, and especially Scandinavia, were demonstrating for the first time the true antiquity of Man and shedding light onto that obscure period of time, prehistory, where written sources could throw no light, or give only a distorted image. Light too was being shed upon historical periods by the critical transliteration or translation of documents and the exploration of the relationship between those documents and archaeological or architectural material. For a brief while, scholars could be expert in many different disciplines, as is exemplified by the career of Thomas Wright, Wroxeter's first excavator (**5**).

Time has not dealt kindly with Wright who has been described by Dr Joan Evans, medievalist and former President of the Society of Antiquaries, as a 'Grub-Street medievalist, always in a hurry, always inexact, always full of energy, combining a genuine love of the Middle Ages with the necessity of earning his living by writing about them in any fashion that would bring him a living'. His primary contribution to antiquarian studies is in the field of Anglo-Saxon literature since he spent a considerable degree of time in translating Anglo-Saxon documents, relating the words to their Latin and English equivalents, collating this material to produce his *Anglo-Saxon Vocabularies*, a book still of value to modern scholars of the language. In that age of polymaths, Wright was also a noted commentator on archaeological matters to numerous British, French and German societies.

Undoubtedly his main contribution to the archaeological world, however, was as a populariser, most notably through his books *Wanderings of an Antiquary*, a sort of archaeological travelogue around the British Isles, and *The Celt, The Roman and The Saxon*, a popular book which ran to three editions but which today is notorious for his attack in the introduction on the newly-developed theory of prehistoric technological progression from the use of stone, then bronze, and then iron tools. Typically, his attack rests more on bluff, derision, and dismissal rather than any coherent refutation through analysis of the remains from prehistoric sites. The rest of the book was, however, a reasonable summary of what was then known of the archaeology of the British Isles before 1066 and drew together many useful illustrations. Wright's achievements and skills lay, therefore, in selling archaeology to the general public, a public which, moreover, was becoming increasingly aware of and interested in the history around it. This interest was fostered by a number of social factors and events which came together in the mid-nineteenth century to encourage the development of historical studies. Most obvious among these was Darwinism which, once accepted, allowed people to perceive that societies evolve, with the perfection of the Victorian state obviously representing the ideal summit of human achievement. The mechanism of evolution could, of course, be translated almost directly into archaeological studies, especially in prehistory (despite Wright's resistance to the idea) in a way that all could appreciate and identify with.

The technological development and rapid spread of the railway across Britain was also a major factor in the promotion of archaeology. Not only could people at all levels of society easily and cheaply visit archaeological sites, a privilege up till then only available to the wealthy and leisured, they could also begin to appreciate regional differences which until then had been unnoticed. The inevitable reaction to this was to want to stress one's own identity, hence the foundation of the many county archaeological societies which still flourish today. This regional pride (which extended to national pride in the foundation of institutions like the Victoria and Albert Museum and in the promotion of national rather than classical, near-eastern or Egyptian, antiquities in the British Museum) meant that increasingly interest was being focused on the antiquities of Roman Britain, the material expression of Britain's relationship with the Roman Empire, itself inevitably inviting comparison with the British Empire. What had life been like when Britain was under Roman rule? Was it possible to match the surviving historical texts of Tacitus, Caesar, and others, to the tangible remains of Roman life in the country? The desire to know more about Britain's past under Roman rule became almost insatiable, leading inevitably to the systematic campaigns to excavate large areas within the abandoned cities of Silchester in Hampshire and Caerwent in south Wales by the end of the century.

Wroxeter too was caught up in the movement through the work of Thomas Wright. He, although not a native of Shropshire, had lived for most of his early life in Ludlow, whose history he later wrote, before taking a degree at Cambridge and then moving to London to earn his living as a freelance archaeological and historical writer. His first visit to Wroxeter seems to have been in the early 1850s when he wrote to an acquaintance about the wealth of archaeological material to be found there. Charles Roach Smith also seems to have visited at roughly the same time, writing up his observations and especially the Jupiter Column fragments in the third volume of his privately-published series *Collectanea Antiqua*. Late in 1858, Wright called on Ludlow's M.P., Beriah Botfield, himself an antiquarian writer, and persuaded him of the need to excavate at Wroxeter. The funds for the enterprise were to be raised from public subscription. The response was swift and £120 was raised by the end of the year, which enabled work to begin on 3 February 1859. From Wright's prolific letters, it is clear that he rarely visited the diggings, leaving the supervision of the farm labourers on the site to a local man, Dr Henry Johnson, who fortunately seems to have been a diligent observer. Wright only appeared on site when he knew that people of importance were to be there or when colleagues wanted to see the site.

Wright's first excavation was, inevitably, in front of the doorway in the Old Work where a deep hole was excavated to examine the foundations of the wall, which proved to descend 14ft (4.3m) below ground surface, much to Wright's astonishment. From there, trenches were dug out radiating away from the north side of the wall until foundations were discovered. Lengths of wall or foundation could then be followed to trace the plan of the building. Gradually, the outline of the great baths basilica was established but, due to the fact Wright was rarely on site, errors crept into the plan of the building which unfortunately led to misconceptions about the basilica. The most important of these was the idea that the south aisle, which lay between the Old Work and the main body of the building, was an open corridor and that thus the rest of the building was physically isolated from the rest of the baths. Before this could be resolved, Wright fell out with the tenant farmer on whose land he was digging, leading to acrimonious arguments and, eventually, to Wright and his diggers being ejected from the field so that the tenant could plant it with turnips. Wright was naturally incensed by the tenant's actions. In a letter to Joseph Mayer, one of his sponsors, he wrote 'We have had a tremendous row with that abominable tenant and his horrible field. I wish he were crammed with turnips till he burst!'. Wright emerged triumphant when the landowner, the Duke of Cleveland, took up his cause and allowed digging to continue on the other side of the Old Work. The farmer, meanwhile, got back to growing turnips, but not before robbing much of the exposed stonework in time-honoured fashion. Wright's workmen were rewarded for their labours in the spectacular discoveries found on the south side of the Old Work and over the next few months they cleared the unheated and warm rooms of the main baths, all of the western suite, part of the eastern suite, the latrine, the shops in front of them, and some of the rooms of the *macellum*.

The preservation of the remains was extraordinary, attracting publicity in the *Illustrated London News* and in a visit by, among others, Charles Dickens, whose article 'Rome and Turnips' for his own magazine *All the Year Round*, bears clear reference to the obviously by now well-known story of Wright's clash with the farmer. The sheer numbers visiting the site, who would be guided round the ruins by local volunteers, prompted the production of a guide book by Wright which ran to seven editions in as many years. In the second edition of this an advertisement by a well-known photographer, Mr Bedford, for a set of eight stereoscopic photographs of the excavations, indicates just how famous the site had become, and incidentally in themselves provide an invaluable record of what Wright actually uncovered. These are almost certainly the earliest photographs of any archaeological excavation taken in Britain and show just how complete and well-preserved the remains were, as can be seen in comparable views of the ruins today (**6, 7**). The deterioration of the site left open to the elements was rapid. Wright was particularly upset by a party of miners on a day-trip from Cannock who visited the site with their families and pushed over most of the tile-stacks (*pilae*) taking some for souvenirs, but most of the destruction was caused by frost and rain rather than visitors.

Among Wright's best-known discoveries was the famous 'old man in the hypocaust', the crouched burial of a man found in the warm room of the western suite, probably a burial of the sub-Roman period rather than the more lurid interpretation presented by Wright who saw the body as that of a poor unfortunate who crawled into the hypocaust to escape the Anglo-Saxon pillage of the city and who had died there alone and terrified. The image was a powerful one and has remained with us: it is unlikely to be true but coloured the morbid and melancholy interpretations of artists, poets, and visitors for years to come. In the light of these and other discoveries, it was almost inevitable that the site should be left open to public inspection. Eventually the landowner agreed, with the administration of the site being left to the Shropshire Natural History and Archaeological Society.

6 *Francis Bedford's photograph of the ruins of the baths as excavated in 1859 or 1860. The view is from the eastern baths suite, looking west*

Gradually, Wright's attention moved away from the Old Work down to the medieval village and the city's rampart which he trenched extensively in its best-preserved section, the glebe lands, finding the clay core of the rampart still standing to an impressive height before turning his attentions to the village itself. Here he excavated the possible site of Wroxeter's 'castle' (almost certainly the Manor house, see **73**), and a cemetery in the same field containing twenty burials. The skulls recovered from these graves proved the subject of much speculation about the health of Wroxeter's former citizens but their strange squashed appearance was almost certainly the result of soil pressure rather than any deformity in life. Further investigations were also carried out on the defences on the northern and eastern side of the city, and in particular at the presumed sites of the gateways. The diggings also extended outside the city walls at these locations in search of Wroxeter's cemeteries. Extensive trenching found the remains of several cremations still in their urns, one associated with a set of surgeon's

7 *A modern view from the same position as the previous figure to show the losses since 1859*

tools, and the base of a tombstone with an elaborate epitaph. Wright's final season of excavation, in 1867, was timed to coincide with the visit of the British Association to Shrewsbury and was wholly sponsored by his friend, the Liverpool businessman Joseph Mayer, at a cost to the latter of £50. Clearly, the impetus behind the excavations was beginning to flag, as was Wright's health, and the investigation of the baths latrine and drain proved to be his last.

In the same year the first popular account of the site, *The Roman Town of Uriconium*, appeared. It had been written by a local man, John Corbett Anderson, but this was no more than a pot-boiler, largely culled from Wright's numerous articles on the site and the various editions of his guide book. Eventually, Wright himself drew together all his material relating to the site and his work there and in 1872 published *Uriconium. An account of the Ancient Roman City at Wroxeter*, which only appeared in print three years before his death. The work is patchy and, far from being a book solely on Wroxeter, reflects all that was then known about Shropshire under Roman rule. As an account of the excavations it is both difficult to read and misses out much information which he or his colleagues had published previously. Wright's work at Wroxeter was important for clarifying much of the historical outline of the city's history and produced a great body of artefacts and information, but much of the context of this material was lost. The fact that he saw little of the remains actually being dug undermines the value of his account. More serious is the sheer speed of excavation, a fact which may be judged from the fact that the *Illustrated London News* account of the excavations shows a fully excavated site only four months after the excavation had started. Clearly, this was little more than site clearance designed solely to uncover walls rather than understand how the site had evolved.

8 *A portrait of J.P. Bushe-Fox, Chief Inspector of Ancient Monuments*

For the rest of the nineteenth century, there was little work carried on in the city, the only exceptions being the work of G. E. Fox who carried out small-scale excavations in the baths in 1896–7, and the work of Charles Darwin. The great scientist, a native of Shrewsbury but by then living in Kent, had become intrigued as to how archaeological remains got buried. His studies led him to deduce that much of the burial was achieved through earthworms burrowing into the ground and casting soil onto the surface. He proved this by determining the depth of humus at Wroxeter, Silchester, and other Roman sites and calculating how much soil had accumulated over the ruins since the Roman period. The results formed part of his study published as *The Formation of Vegetable Mould through the Action of Worms* (1881), a natural history of the earthworm and its role in soil improvement which is still a classic work.

The purpose of Fox's work was to clarify the structural sequence of the buildings as uncovered by Wright, and to record properly the walls and other remains that he had found. Further excavation was complicated by the huge spoil heaps which still dominated and comprehensively covered parts of the site. Fox's work, as might be expected of someone heavily involved in excavating the Roman city at Silchester in Hampshire, was very competent, consisting of shrewdly placed trenches to observe key relationships between walls and individual rooms. As a result, he recorded many valuable details about the site which have since then been lost through further weathering or during consolidation of the remains.

This brief examination of the ruins failed to spark any more activity on the site. By the early twentieth century the Shropshire Archaeological Society was lamenting the lack of progress at Wroxeter, comparing the rudimentary state of knowledge with the comprehensive and spectacular excavations in Silchester which had been funded and carried out by the Society of Antiquaries of London. Eventually, more money was raised and a series of excavations began on the field towards the village and across the road from the baths site. The site was directed by J. P. Bushe-Fox, one of Britain's leading archaeologists and at that time Chief Inspector of Ancient Monuments (**8**). As with the excavations at Silchester, the method of excavation adopted was to dig parallel trenches until stone footings or mortared walls were found upon which the trenches could then be opened out into an area excavation. The first season, in 1912, largely drew a blank as there had been much disturbance of this area by later houses from Wroxeter village (and the spot chosen may also have coincided with the building excavated by Thomas Telford). Soon, however, the regularly-spaced plans of buildings began to emerge with their colonnaded street fronts and concrete floors (see **42**). Interestingly, the walls, which must have been of timber, were barely noticed, the buildings being recognised more by their floors. This supports the view that if there had been timber buildings overlying the stone-built ones, Bushe-Fox would not have noticed them. The next two seasons, 1913–4, were also very successful with the temple being found in the first year along with the neighbouring building complex known as Site VI whose excavation was completed in the following season. This last season was cut short by the events of August 1914 which put paid to any further work at Wroxeter for another generation. It is indeed sobering to realise that of Bushe-Fox's five student diggers in 1913 only one, Sir Mortimer Wheeler, returned from the Western Front, a fact that Wheeler himself found difficult to cope with. Later, in his autobiography, *Still Digging*, he commented that his generation had 'been blotted out' leaving the few survivors with 'a sense of isolation', a feeling 'which became a dominant element' in his own life.

9 *An aerial photograph of the baths site in 1928. Note the spoil heaps covering large parts of the site with the custodian's house and site museum at bottom right*

The excavations at Wroxeter had a great impact on the public imagination despite their relatively modest achievements. We know that Wilfred Owen, who lived in nearby Shrewsbury, cycled out to the site often with his brother, and was inspired to compose his ode *Uriconium*. H. Lang Jones was also inspired to write a series of poems, published as the slim volume *Songs of a Buried City* (1913). Earlier, in 1896, A.E. Housman had published *A Shropshire Lad*, a collection which includes the poem *On Wenlock Edge*, a masterly evocation of the transience of life in the light of the fate of the city. The poem may have been stimulated by his visit to the site two years previously. But perhaps the most evocative poem relating to Wroxeter is that by Mary Webb, who had been born only five miles from the site in 1881. She wrote two pieces of work on Wroxeter, a poem *Viroconium* (*see* frontispiece) written in 1924, and an essay, *The Return of the Romans: a Dream of Uriconium*, written the year before for a local society.

The excavations that had inspired her were those carried out on the forum by Donald Atkinson from 1923. He had begun in the same field as that excavated by Bushe-Fox but had started immediately opposite the baths site and close to the farm labourer's cottages that occupy the corner of that field. Again, his method consisted of trenching and area clearance on the discovery of walls but often the published photographs leave one with the impression that the work was carried out hurriedly and without much attention to detail, despite the remarkable evidence he uncovered. This shows most clearly in his photographs of the extraordinary find of samian and *mortaria* bowls lying as they fell in the gutter (**30**). The poor cleaning and definition of the finds make it almost impossible to pick them out from the background. Nonetheless, Atkinson had a good grasp of the architectural details of the site, and in particular of the parallels for what he quickly recognised as a forum with an unfinished baths block beneath, even if in detail his overall reconstruction of the plan can be questioned. The forum inscription, diploma, and mirror (**colour plate 18**) were accorded due prominence in the final publication, as might be expected of someone of his classical training, but his methods were not subtle enough to deal with the timber buildings of the early and late phases of the site's history whose remains he noted but did not understand. Atkinson also, like Wright, took a wider view of the city and excavated a number of trenches across the ramparts and in the eastern cemetery. In the latter enterprise he was rewarded with a number of cremations but found that many others had recently been destroyed by ploughing.

Atkinson's work acted as a spur to further excavation within the city, although given the economic depression only small-scale work was possible, funded largely by Sir Charles Marston, president of the Shropshire Archaeological Society. He initially financed excavations in the late 1920s to early 1930s at the putative location of the bridge across the Severn in the village, on a kiln just beyond the north-western gate, and on the public latrine next to the baths, all of which were directed by John Morris, a local amateur archaeologist. After Morris' death, Kathleen Kenyon, later to become a Dame for her work at Jericho, was funded to carry out further work on the baths. The aim was to remove some of the unsightly spoil heaps and examine the more crucial relationships between the walls on the site with a general view to improving both the appearance and understanding of the site (**9**). To this end she opened a number of trenches within the baths but was also able to explore the baths basilica for the first time in nearly a century. Her techniques and abilities were better than those of Bushe-Fox and Atkinson but limited time and funds meant that she could achieve little, being only able to dig a number of small trenches. The unfortunate consequence of this, especially in the case of the basilica, was that she did not appreciate fully the complexities of the site. For example, in digging at the east end of the nave she was only able to observe the rubble platforms of the sub-Roman rebuilding in section, where she could not understand what she was seeing (see chapter 7). This led her to conclude that the rubble layer was merely the collapse of the basilica's walls rather than the important evidence for post-Roman occupation that it in fact represented. Her long sections across the site found the gravel street but did not understand its purpose – on her sections it is labelled as a 'speckly ?late disturbance'. Despite these drawbacks, her work did advance understanding, and especially dating, of the site allowing her to outline a sequence of the bath's development. A certain amount of new digging also took place within the baths themselves; for instance, new rooms were located in the eastern baths suite, but generally the work was small-scale and piecemeal which led her to a number of erroneous conclusions. The most important of these was the perpetuation of the false impression that the south aisle of the basilica was not originally part of that building and that thus the baths and basilica had started out as separate entities. She believed that this came about because the baths had originally been intended to be a forum rather than a bath house, in the same way that on the other side of the road the unfinished baths had been replaced by the forum, and that at some point a decision had been made to change the position of both baths and forum to their opposite locations. From the evidence of the latest excavations this is now thought to be unlikely but did initially colour the interpretations of Dr Graham Webster in particular. Dame Kathleen also took the opportunity to cut a number of sections across the city defences which showed their true sequence of development, including the legionary phase, even if she did not fully realise what she had found.

The intervention of the Second World War prevented any further digging, the site being used as the base for a searchlight battery to protect the nearby 8th Army Air Force airfield at Atcham, about a mile to the north. The lights themselves were not positioned on the site but lay in the fields to the south although barrack blocks were established among the spoil tips within the ruins. Their only moment of glory was to pinpoint a bomber which was returning from an abortive raid on Liverpool. The aircraft dropped its load in the glebe fields near the present day Wroxeter Hotel where its bomb crater can still be seen. After 1945, the site had been handed back to the Shropshire Archaeological Society in a very run-down condition. American bulldozers, left behind from the airfield construction, permitted swift tidying up of the site, which in 1947 passed from the society's control to the Ministry of Works. The event was commemorated in a visit to the society's AGM by Baillie Reynolds, the local Inspector of Ancient Monuments, whose keynote address entitled 'The Future of Wroxeter' promised that the Ministry 'intended to expose one complete *insula*' and to investigate the underlying early deposits before the site was consolidated for the public. Prophetically, he warned the society against expecting early results which, given that it has taken 50 years to achieve this aim, seems a masterly understatement.

The tidying up of the site was achieved but the promised excavations themselves failed to materialise for five years. Then, in 1952, Dame Kathleen returned to Wroxeter to carry out a training excavation on the site of a large house south of the baths. She was ably assisted in her teaching and supervision by Dr Graham Webster who, in 1954, was asked by Baillie Reynolds to take on the excavation of the public baths. This work started in 1955 but had been preceded by the work of the masons who, in consolidating the remains, inadvertently removed some important information about the inter-relationships of the various walls. Initially, Graham Webster's approach was to dig quite small trenches in key positions, as had Fox and Kenyon before him but soon, as the spoil heaps vanished, a different style of excavation was adopted. This involved laying out a regular grid of boxes separated by standing sections (baulks), a technique of excavation devised by Sir Mortimer Wheeler to allow the relationships between features and layers to be seen in both area and section at the same time. The excavations were once again carried out as training digs under the aegis of the University of Birmingham Extra-Mural Department but also increasingly used volunteer and, at times, prison labour to clear larger areas.

By the mid-1960s, most of the ruins of the baths had been cleared and the outlines of the buildings were understood so that attention turned instead to the indoor and outdoor exercise areas (that is the *palaestra* and baths basilica respectively), and the market hall (*macellum*). Work on the latter had been delayed as the site custodian's house and a Nissen hut that was the site's museum had been built over it but these modern buildings were now demolished so that the work could proceed. The excavation of these

North-South Street and Frontages · Interpretation Phase Y2

Scale
0   1   2   3 *metres*

?out-buildings

Cobble street

10 *An interpretation of the evidence for Building 1, baths basilica site. The building has bowed sides made of timbers set on the ground, and must therefore have had a hipped roof. Internally, it is divided into three distinct areas by partitions: a clay floor (A5), a hard-standing made of four square areas packed with vertically-set smashed tile (A6), and a fragmentary cobbled area (A19). The pits seen in* **25** *lie between this building and the wall at the left*

areas took the site in new and unexpected directions. Graham Webster's work on the *macellum* and *palaestra* soon encountered the remains of the legionary fortress beneath the public buildings and eventually allowed a clearer understanding of the relationship between the military and civilian phases of the site.

Work on the baths basilica was started in two separate areas in 1966. On the main body of the building, a large trench was opened up using prisoners from Drake Hall, Staffordshire, who soon reached the floor of the building where it was noted that there were a number of substantial postholes cutting into the floor. This was evidence of a major building which had been erected after the baths basilica had been demolished, whose existence had been hitherto unsuspected. In the same year one of the present authors (Philip Barker), who was then acting as Graham Webster's assistant, was asked to investigate a 'blank' area well beyond the baths so that foundations for the new custodian's house could be excavated. His work, again with prison labour and a few volunteers, astonishingly produced a remarkable bow-sided building (Building 1) with a tile hard-standing whose appearance was more medieval than Romano-British, but which analysis has lately shown was probably built in the later third or perhaps fourth century (**10**). In the next year, Philip Barker was able to establish that two other similar buildings lay beneath the first and that they were associated with a complex of industrial

27

11 *An aerial photograph of the* insulae *north of the baths. The Bell brook is visible at (a) with, below and to the right, the diagonal line of the early defences (b). A large rectangular blank area (c), outlined by a pale parchmark, is the suggested site of the* forum boarium. *Between these two features are a number of substantial town houses, one with a Y-shaped hypocaust (d). A single dark parchmark, the line of the legionary fortress ditch, can be seen running beneath the* forum boarium *and the town houses (e-f)*

pits perhaps related to tanning or fulling (see **25**). Clearly, there was still a considerable amount of archaeology on the baths basilica site and wholesale clearance was not the answer. Accordingly, he was asked to direct excavations on the baths basilica site while Graham Webster continued to excavate the baths and *macellum*.

The approach adopted on the baths basilica site owed more to techniques developed on medieval sites where the buildings although often large had insubstantial foundations, unlike the massive masonry buildings of Roman Britain. It was decided to clear the site at the same horizon over the whole area, rather than excavating in small boxes. The advantage of this technique, known as area excavation, was that it became possible to observe the spatial patterns of buildings and surfaces which had been in use at the same time. Furthermore, features that might not appear significant in isolation in the bottom of a box-trench could be given due prominence when seen in relation to other features. Graham Webster too adopted these new techniques where he was able to do so, but his working areas were inevitably much more confined given that he was constrained by the standing walls of the baths themselves.

Whilst excavations were undertaken on the baths complex with a view to their public display, the rest of the city saw little new work. The excavations of both Bushe-Fox and Atkinson had been completely reburied, with the exception of the colonnade of the forum. A number of small-scale excavations were carried out on an independent basis by a local amateur archaeologist, the late Dr John Houghton. Some of these produced important results, such as the tilery and pottery kiln adjacent to the River Severn, a glass-working site in the village, a city house in the south-east quarter, a cistern by the defences, and a possible quay associated with the Claudian fort south of Wroxeter. He also sectioned the defences in a number of locations and recorded the last vestiges of the eastern cemetery along the Watling Street between the city rampart and the Horseshoe public house. To these may be added the excavations of other archaeologists including Dr Stephen Johnson's re-excavation of Dame Kathleen Kenyon's trench through the eastern defences in 1975–6 which located the legionary defences on the east side of the fortress, and latterly Dr Simon Esmonde Cleary's excavation in 1991–2 on the north-eastern corner of the defences which examined the suggested position of a bastion identified from the air by Dr Arnold Baker. Within the city, renewal of modern sewerage services involved the re-excavation of the forum drain so that a sewer pipe could be laid inside it, an excavation which once again allowed a glimpse of the archaeology of the forum colonnade. This work, carried out by Gill Hey and Peter Brown of the Central Archaeological Services of the Department of Environment, made the major discovery of the city defences on the western, riverbank, side, disproving the theory that there had been erosion of the cliff edge here. The city defences had also been sectioned in 1960 by Graham Webster who had earlier studied the course and surviving remains of the aqueduct just before it was bulldozed for ploughing. The same fate also befell the rampart running along the crest of the Bell Brook valley but fortunately the city ramparts themselves remained unscathed, although they were constantly being diminished by repeated ploughing. Indeed, ploughing had become the major threat to the city from the mid-1960s since the land was still down to arable cultivation. One side effect of this, however, was that the city's interior began to produce splendid crop- and parch-marks of the underlying streets and buildings (**11**).

That such evidence had been seen before is not in doubt, as was demonstrated in the eighteenth century by Mr Clayton who had known where to dig to obtain stone, and also by Bushe-Fox's plan of the city's streets observed during a dry summer while digging there. After the Second World War, however, the greater availability of trained personnel, good-quality cameras, and cheap war-surplus aircraft led to a rapid growth and development in aerial archaeology. Initially, the pioneer over Wroxeter's airspace was J. K. St Joseph, founder of the Cambridge University Committee for Aerial Archaeology (CUCAP), whose discovery of a city house has already been mentioned. Soon other, more locally-based pilots took over, notably Dr Arnold Baker and Jim Pickering (both flying from the late 1950s onwards) and latterly Chris Musson of

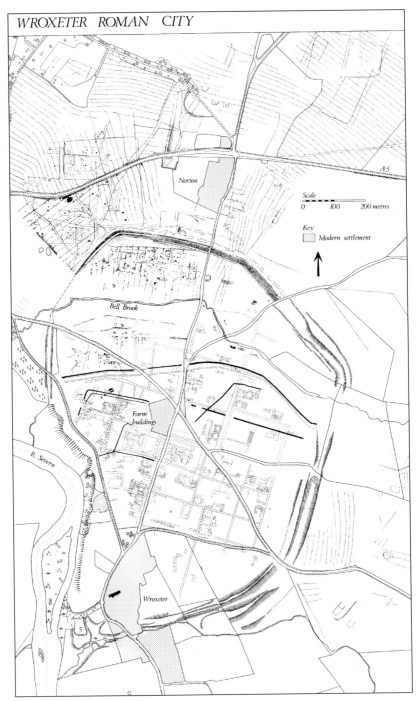

12 *The plan of the city drawn up from aerial photographs. The large, stone-built town houses are prominent in the city centre but the outlying areas seem to be sparsely settled. On the northern side of the city, and outside its defences, are the sinuous lines characteristic of medieval ridge-and-furrow ploughing. These overlie a mass of earlier features (see* **32***)*

Clwyd-Powys Archaeological Trust and then CADW. The contribution of Dr Arnold Baker to our understanding of Wroxeter cannot be overestimated. His photographs are of extraordinary clarity, showing the individual rooms within houses and sometimes even the remains of underfloor heating within them. His concerted campaign over twenty years of regular flying enabled an almost complete coverage of the city to be achieved which, allied with the amazingly clear set of vertical photographs taken by CUCAP in the dry summer of 1975, allowed a new city plan to be drawn up by Dr David Wilson of CUCAP, which, with additions by Philip Barker and others, has remained the principal plan of the site until recently enhanced by the geophysical survey of 1995-7 (**12**).

In a way, the great clarity of the aerial photographs was in itself misleading, encouraging acceptance that the buildings seen were the total picture of settlement rather than just those which are more responsive to the soil conditions. Those working on the city knew that this was not the case, however, but the image could only begin to be corrected once the geophysical survey of the city got underway (see chapter 5). This is the first time that such a battery of techniques has been used on a complex urban site, and also represents the largest geophysical survey undertaken. The results have far exceeded expectations and it is no exaggeration to state that they have revolutionised our thinking about the density of settlement in Roman cities in Britain (**colour plate 3**). For the first time, the true extent and nature of occupation within the city can be accurately gauged, even though without excavation the date of individual buildings, and their duration, is impossible to establish. Even more important is the fact that excavation will certainly add even more buildings to the total as was proved on the baths basilica site where excavations found not just the public building, but an additional 70 buildings. None of these had been seen in aerial photographs, including the basilica itself. Even with the imperfect picture provided by the geophysical survey, it is clear that the overall density of occupation means that the accepted picture of Wroxeter as an under-populated city, or even as a failure, is certainly incorrect. Running parallel with the geophysical survey has been the Wroxeter Hinterland Project itself. This was formulated to elucidate the pattern and depth of Romanization within the landscape around Wroxeter, and thus put what is known about the city into its social and economic context. The results of both the geophysical survey and the Wroxeter Hinterland Project have revolutionised our picture of the area, and of the *Cornovii* in general, so that they can be placed within the larger framework of Roman Britain.

What made the survey possible was the decision taken by the government in the mid-1970s to purchase the bulk of the land enclosed within Wroxeter's ramparts. Much of the remainder lies within the care of The National Trust. The purchased land is presently administered by English Heritage on behalf of the Department of the Environment. The importance of this far-sighted decision cannot be overstated. At a stroke, ploughing of the site has stopped, protecting the underlying fragile archaeological layers. Furthermore, the site is protected from development so that archaeological research can carry on at a suitably slow and considered pace, turning it into the largest archaeological laboratory in the world. This should be contrasted with much of present-day archaeology in Britain which is currently driven largely by developer-funding.

2 Wroxeter under military rule AD 47-90

The Roman conquest of the territory of the *Cornovii*, within which the site of Wroxeter lay, appears to have been swiftly accomplished leaving barely a trace in the historical record. It seems probable that this is because the tribe submitted immediately and without substantial loss of life. Nevertheless, for the local inhabitants it must initially have been an overwhelming and terrifying experience. In order to understand why the conquest will have had this effect, it is perhaps necessary to explain something of what is known of the tribe.

From the Roman geographer Ptolemy we know that the tribe of the *Cornovii* occupied a large territory which later included the Roman settlements of Wroxeter and Chester. It thus seems likely that the whole of modern Shropshire and Cheshire should be seen as the core territory, although it may have extended eastwards into Staffordshire and Warwickshire and westwards into the eastern Welsh hills, such as the Clwydian range and the Berwyns (**13**). This area has a coherent geographical unity consisting of extensive lowlands, the Cheshire and north Shropshire plains with the Severn valley, which are surrounded by substantial hills and areas of high ground on the western, southern, and eastern sides. To the north, it is likely that the Mersey formed a frontier with the *Brigantes*, and that the Wirral was included within Cornovian territory. (Perhaps it was this projecting block of land that gave the 'horn' (*Cornu-*) element to the tribal name.) It can be seen that the territory was largely land-locked, the only access to the sea being via the River Severn, which passed through the territory of the *Dobunni* to the south, and by the Rivers Mersey and Dee which flow either side of the Wirral peninsula. It seems probable that this northern route, the only one over which the tribe had sole control, was its principal trade route. Evidence for this comes from discoveries at the ancient port of Meols, situated at the north-western extremity of the Wirral, which has produced a comprehensive range of finds indicating a long-lived and important settlement. Sadly, the site has been eroding steadily into the sea since the sixteenth century and our knowledge of it is limited to stray finds collected largely in the mid-nineteenth century.

Among this collection, however, are items of exceptional interest including a number of silver coins of the *Coriosolites*, an Iron Age tribe who lived on the Armorican peninsula (now part of Brittany), and even some silver Carthaginian coins. Their discovery at Meols strongly suggests that the site was an *emporium*, a trading settlement similar to the better-known one at Hengistbury Head in Dorset. Clearly, traders were making the long

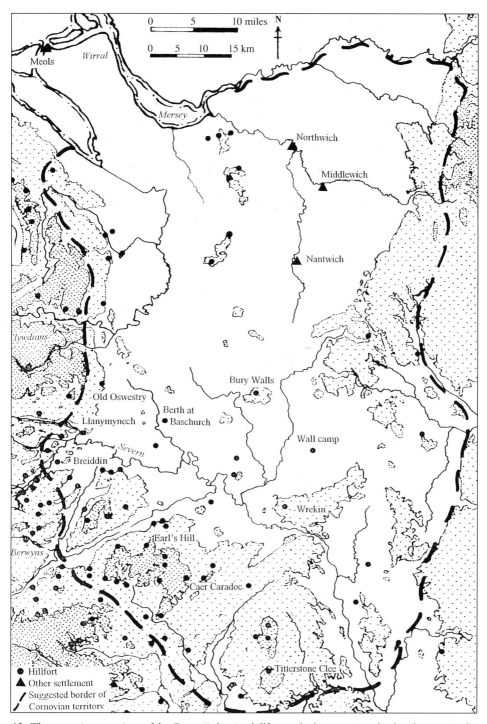

13 *The approximate territory of the Cornovii showing hillforts and other prominent landmarks mentioned in the text*

14 *Old Oswestry hillfort from the north with Oswestry beyond. The fort's western entrance is dominated by a number of rectangular enclosures of unknown use*

journey to the site to trade with the *Cornovii* though what they were taking away in return remains a mystery. Agricultural products are a strong possibility since Cornovian territory has good-quality farm land and the area is especially rich in pasture for livestock. Equally, the *Cornovii* had other resources including extensive deposits of copper and lead (although there is no evidence that they extensively exploited the latter), and they had control of three of the four inland brine springs of Britain, at Middlewich, Nantwich and Northwich. This trade was very important, since salt is an essential commodity for life as well as being used in processing leather and cloth and for the salting of meat and the production of cheese.

Of these resources only salt is traceable archaeologically since Iron Age salt production involved its storage and transportation in large, crudely-made earthenware jars. Examination of the distribution of these jars has shown an interesting pattern, with the middle Iron Age distribution being focused within the Cornovian heartland whilst its competitor, salt jars from Droitwich, dominated the lower Severn Valley and South Shropshire. By the late Iron Age, however, the Droitwich salt jars were used only in their core territory whilst Cheshire took over as the main supplier of salt within eastern Wales and along the entire length of the Welsh coastline, even penetrating as far southward as the estuary of the Severn, the natural heartland of Droitwich salt. The distribution of Cheshire salt jars thus implies that the *Cornovii* successfully marketed their salt at the expense of that of their neighbours, the *Dobunni*, even within the latter's home territory.

This success could be taken as evidence for the strong control by the Cornovian aristocracy over the important salt trade, which in turn may have led to an increasing degree of centralisation within Cornovian society. If so, then this is at variance with the common understanding of that society which tends to view the tribe as politically fragmented, an argument based upon the large number of hillforts within Cornovian territory, each of which has been interpreted as representing the power-base of a chieftain. In addition, it has often been argued that the low number, and poor quality, of finds recovered on Cornovian sites indicates that the tribe was poor. In fact, their level of material culture is more like that of the middle Iron Age than that of the late Iron Age. This poverty of material culture becomes more and more evident as the tribes of the south and east, already developing distinct tribal identities through differences in pottery decoration and shapes, in the production of distinctive metalwork traditions in iron and bronze, and in the use and production of coinage, became wealthier through contacts with the Roman world after the conquest of Gaul by Caesar.

The developments in the south and east of Britain have led archaeologists to view these late Iron Age societies as becoming increasingly sophisticated and complex in the pre-Roman period. The further implication of this is that those areas, largely in the west and north of Britain, that do not exhibit these tendencies must be relatively culturally, if not socially, 'poor'. Implicit in this argument is the idea that wealth in Iron Age societies was expressed primarily in terms of material goods. Of course, if wealth is understood only in these terms then the *Cornovii* would appear poor in comparison with the tribes of the south and east. We would argue instead that, due to its inland position, Cornovian culture could never be stimulated to develop in the way that happened in those areas close to the continent. Since its territory lay a considerable distance from the sea, and therefore difficult to approach from any direction, and the major trade routes from the south were controlled by a rival tribe, the *Dobunni*, it seems that the *Cornovii* were not able to use what wealth they had to acquire prestigious imported goods. Instead, they seem to have measured wealth and status in other ways – for example through the ownership of livestock or land – rather than in material objects. If this was the case, then the large number of hillforts within their territory may merely reflect the tribe's wealth rather than its insecurity or political fragmentation. There are certainly plenty of anthropological parallels for societies that do not measure wealth in material goods, and the *Cornovii* may well have taken this route, albeit because they had no opportunity to acquire material wealth. Certainly, any argument that Cornovian territory was poor can no longer be sustained. Both Shropshire and Cheshire are rich agricultural areas, particularly in pasture, and there is increasing evidence that much of the landscape had been cleared for agriculture by the early Iron Age, as shown by the pollen record and the profusion of enclosures discovered by aerial photography in the lowland areas.

The extent of lowland settlement in Cornovian territory has only been appreciated in the last few years, and has thrown a fresh perspective on the better-known, and better-preserved, hillforts of the region. Too few of the low-lying enclosures have been excavated to a satisfactory level to draw substantial conclusions about their function or even their dates but enough is known to show that many started in the Iron Age and continued in occupation into the Roman period. There must have been a range of functions for these enclosures; certainly there is a range of forms and conceivably there was a relationship between form and function. Some were livestock compounds since they have attached droveways, still others appear to be linked with field systems implying that they are farmsteads. What is now becoming clearer is that a substantial element of the population, if not the greater part, lived in these enclosures rather than the hillforts. If this was indeed the case, what was the function of the hillforts? Again, too few of these have been adequately excavated to enable a ready answer to be given but a close examination of the sites shows that the term covers a multitude of types and that their varying sizes and locations strongly suggest that they too had differing functions. A number of the more exposed sites, such as the Wrekin or Titterstone Clee, may well have only been occupied seasonally, perhaps in a form of transhumance, whilst the large, substantial lowland forts such as those at Old Oswestry and Bury Walls are more likely to have been occupied all the year round (**14**). These two forts, with their massive ramparts and ditches and expansive level interiors (both enclose about 20 acres or 8 hectares) are akin to the large hillforts of the south and east and of Wessex, such as Maiden Castle in Dorset. In Wessex and along the south coast such sites were already developing into town-like settlements, often called *oppida* after the term used by Caesar to describe them.

It seems likely that, if any sites within Cornovian territory were developing towards an urban lifestyle before the Roman conquest, then Bury Walls and Old Oswestry are the prime candidates. Another group that may be differentiated from the rest are those located in or near wetlands, such as Wall Camp, or the Berth at Baschurch (**colour plate 22**). These are both sites taking advantage of the abundant wildlife living in the marshes which surround them, whilst still being able to exploit arable or pasture land nearby. Hillforts almost certainly had a religious role too since excavated examples often produce evidence for shrines within the enclosed area. It is possible that the tribe would congregate on hillforts at appropriate times of the year to celebrate specific festivals, on which occasions markets or fairs may have been held. Another characteristic of Shropshire's hillforts is that many of the more substantial are paired with smaller examples on neighbouring hills, as at Earl's Hill, Pontesbury beside which is Pontesford hillfort, or the Breiddin with its adjacent sites at Middletown Hill and New Pieces enclosure. Quite what significance should be attached to these apparent pairings is uncertain. They may represent no more than a progression from a large to a smaller site, or vice-versa, or one may have been separately occupied by the religious or political leaders of the kinship or tribal group. The association of these forts is certainly significant but without more information cannot be explained further.

The profusion of hillforts within the territory must, however, be telling us something of the society that created them. The understandable deduction is that the hillforts imply a violent and aggressive society, each clan within its hillfort protecting itself behind its ramparts, but this may not have been their only function. Similarly, the sheer number of forts has been taken as evidence of the lack of a central political focus within Cornovian society, each hillfort being thought to be the seat of an individual chief and his clan. If so, the tribe would ultimately be no more than a confederation of separate sub-tribes under their individual leaders, each perhaps owing an allegiance to an overlord or 'king'. Economically, this argument has less force. As already shown, the territory has a geographical coherence which might in itself encourage unity, and the archaeological evidence for the salt trade surely bears witness to a centralised approach to marketing this important commodity. If so, we can deduce that Cornovian society was more centralised than first appears, its hillforts representing a form of conspicuous consumption of wealth, whilst undoubtedly providing refuges in times of crisis. The

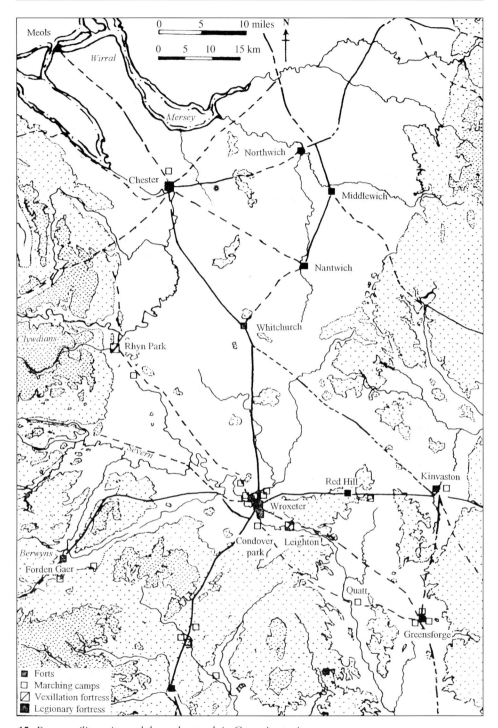

15 *Roman military sites and the road network in Cornovian territory*

37

very fact of their creation must have involved considerable communal effort, which indicates both that a substantial population was available for such work and that a tribal leadership was able to deploy this workforce.

In sum, there is no doubt that Cornovian society was substantially different from those known from the south and east of Britain. It was apparently an inward-looking society since it had few opportunities for easy communication with the outside world. It had a substantial agricultural, probably pastoral, economy but also had considerable mineral resources in the form of copper, iron and salt with probably largely unexploited resources of lead and silver. There seems to be evidence for a developing aristocratic hierarchy living in enclosed farmsteads, often with multiple ditches, and located on lowland and highland but without the customary trappings of large quantities of high-status metalwork or pottery.

Given this background, the arrival of the Roman legions in Cornovian territory in the late 40s ushered in a period of great change. Unfortunately, we know nothing of the details of the conquest, though it is likely that the tribal chief(s) were among the eleven kings, commemorated on Claudius' triumphal arch in Rome, who submitted to the Emperor at Colchester without resisting, despite the fact the tribe lay beyond the immediate area of conquest. Nonetheless there is evidence from the Wrekin hillfort of a violent end to the occupation there in the form of burnt roundhouses and the discovery of two javelin (*pilum*) heads, one from the fort's gate, which suggest that there may have been some resistance. Perhaps the Roman army were making an example of one fort to cow the rest of the tribe since there is little evidence of widespread destruction elsewhere, and after a token resistance at this fort the tribal élite readily submitted in the realisation that siding with Rome brought trading and social advantages.

For the Roman army, skilled as they were in dealing with ill-disciplined Celtic armies, the conquest of Cornovian territory was doubtless a routine affair. It seems reasonably clear that the main force moved into the area along the line north of the Wrekin which later became the Watling Street, but there may have been a smaller force moving along the east bank of the Severn, marching north from the complex of forts at Greensforge in Staffordshire to build a camp at Leighton, some three miles downstream from Wroxeter (**15**). The fort here is of a type known as a vexillation fortress, meaning that the troops within it consisted of detachments of citizen troops (legionaries) and non-Roman (auxiliary) infantry and cavalry to form a campaign force. An early date for this fortress is indicated by a number of Republican silver coins (*denarii*) and early military metalwork known from the site. The close proximity of this fortress to the Wrekin hillfort makes it likely that it served as the base for the storming of the fort. Once resistance was broken, the army will have moved on to complete the campaign, with the Severn probably forming a natural limit to the advance at this initial stage.

It is at this point that the site at Wroxeter seems to have been established. Its naturally-strong position readily attracted the attention of the military. It controlled a good ford across the Severn and had extensive views across the central Shropshire plain and of the passes out of it. The activity of the army in the area is manifested by the large number of Roman forts in and around the later town. Some of these could be interpreted as evidence for a number of separate campaigns though they may be practice forts established once the legionary fortress was in operation. One at least, the small auxiliary fort to the south of the later town, seems to belong to this early period judging by the dating provided by a small-scale excavation there. It was large enough to hold 500 auxiliary troops and was situated to control the ford across the Severn. A possible occupant of this fort is known from a tombstone discovered in the centre of Wroxeter which shows an auxiliary cavalryman, Tiberius Claudius Tirintius, from a Thracian cohort, riding down a naked barbarian (see **22**). His first names indicate that he received his honourable discharge under either Claudius or Nero since it was customary for those who received the grant of citizenship to take the name of the person who bestowed the honour, in this case the Emperor.

The conquest of a new territory by the army involved first the military defeat of the tribe, which might be achieved politically or through full-scale warfare, followed by an occupation in force, the territory being administered directly by the military commander. At this early stage of the Roman conquest, the army was moving and spreading rapidly through lowland Britain, with forts and fortresses being constructed in large numbers, many being occupied only briefly. Whilst on campaign the army constructed temporary marching camps or, for longer campaigns, vexillation fortresses, but once the territory was secured forts of more standardised form and size were established. These were capable of holding either 500 or 1000 auxiliary troops, or were larger legionary fortresses capable of holding a legion of about 5500 citizen troops. It is becoming increasingly clear from the letters and documents recovered from the frontier fort at *Vindolanda*, near Hadrian's Wall, that these auxiliary forts and legionary fortresses were not fully manned except perhaps during the closed campaign season in winter. For much of the time, troops will have been out on patrol or on detachment elsewhere and during the summer months will probably have been on campaign far in advance of their winter quarters.

As already noted, two campaign routes seem to have been used as a pincer movement enclosing the Wrekin. This hill is often thought to be the site of the principal hillfort of the tribe but it may have been chosen for attack since it was easily isolated and was the first major Cornovian hillfort that the Roman army will have encountered. Given its prominence, the taking and burning of the fort there will have sent a huge literal and symbolic smoke-signal to the rest of the tribe, intimidating them and encouraging their surrender. The southern route was that running up the River Severn, on its east bank until it crossed, probably in the vicinity of Quatt near Bridgnorth, to avoid the narrow defile of the Ironbridge Gorge. The route then extended to the site of the vexillation fortress at Leighton, perhaps re-crossing from the bank opposite that site or in the vicinity of Buildwas, about a mile downstream. Part of the campaign force may have continued along the west bank, however, to build the fort recently recognised at Condover Park. The other, northern, line of advance can be postulated extending westwards from the fortress of *legio XIIII* at Mancetter in Warwickshire. This line, the latter-day Watling Street, passed through a number of regularly-spaced forts including those at Kinvaston (*Pennocrucium*), Wall (*Letocetum*) in Staffordshire, and Red Hill (*Uxacona*) in Shropshire before passing to the north of the Wrekin to cross the Severn initially at Atcham. Beyond the Severn, Watling Street extended westwards into what is now central Wales via the forts at Westbury, Forden Gaer and Caersws. Another branch probably progressed up the east bank of the Perry valley to the vexillation fortress at Rhyn Park. This latter fortress seems to have been the base for the final battle against

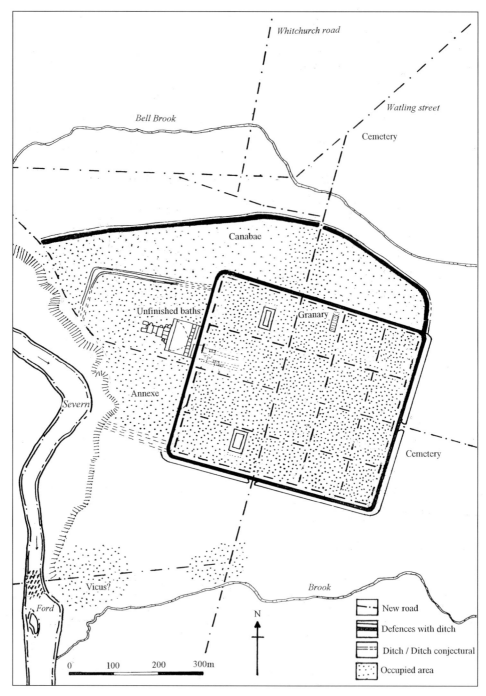

16 *A plan of the legionary fortress at Wroxeter, c.57-90, and its immediate surroundings showing the suggested positions of the* vicus *and* canabae

the British chief Caratacus whose last stand, it has been argued, was made at the huge hillfort at Llanymynech.

The construction of the campaign roads was in itself a major task. The land on either side of the roadway was cleared of trees and bushes and a shallow trench dug into the underlying subsoil. This was then filled with stone and the resulting foundation was then capped with a layer of gravel or occasionally paved according to the local conditions. Where necessary, bridges were constructed to cross narrow streams and on marshy ground the roadway might be raised on a causeway (*agger*). Stretches of these still survive and can be seen today. Ordinarily, roads in the open countryside will also have been provided with drainage ditches on each side.

As fully-completed, the Roman road network centred on Wroxeter. Here, the broad ford across the Severn could be controlled, along with access to the river itself and thus to the river traffic passing up- and downstream. The most important road was undoubtedly the Watling Street which, swinging round in a long curve, approached Wroxeter from the north-east. Initially it by-passed the site of the fortress and made instead for the ford at Atcham. The small auxiliary fort to the south of Wroxeter was thus isolated from this road although it presumably lay upon an earlier, probably prehistoric, route along the east bank of the Severn and it would have been possible to follow this track until it was crossed by the new road at the confluence of the Tern and Severn. At some time in the mid-fifties, and certainly by 57, the foundation of the fortress at Wroxeter meant that a spur road from Watling Street had to be built to link the fortress to the road system, entering by the north gate (**16**). This diversion quickly superseded the more direct westerly route through Atcham. Instead, traffic was routed through the fortress, and later the city, to cross the river at Wroxeter's ford. From there, two main roads are known: a south-western route extending via the Craven Arms gap into Gloucestershire and South Wales, towards the legion controlling the south-west, and a link road which joined up with the existing western route into mid-Wales. The junction of this spur and the main western road was probably at Meole Brace where a roadside settlement was later to grow up. There were also important routes to the north which stayed to the east of the Severn. The primary route was that trending almost due north to *Rutunium* (near Moreton Corbett) and Whitchurch (*Mediolanum*) where the road divided and a north-western arm continued to Chester and the Wirral while a north-eastern branch crossed the Mersey to form the the west coast road. The north-western road towards the copper mine at Llanymynech via the fort at Rhyn Park was extended into the territory of the *Ordovices* and *Deceangli*. The network of auxiliary forts covering Cornovian territory and the establishment of the roads between them cannot have been achieved overnight and it is likely that this was accomplished during the 60s when little active campaigning is known.

The reactions of both natives and Romans to the conquest must have been vastly different. For the Roman soldiers, there was nothing unusual about the area and their discipline would have ensured an ordered approach to the territory. Resistance would have been ruthlessly dealt with, but equally they were not out to create trouble and it must be assumed that the local population were fairly if perhaps roughly treated. For some of the tribe the whole experience can only have been traumatic. This is particularly true of those who lived in and around the areas requisitioned by the army for the construction of fortifications who will have been dispossessed of their land. Such a

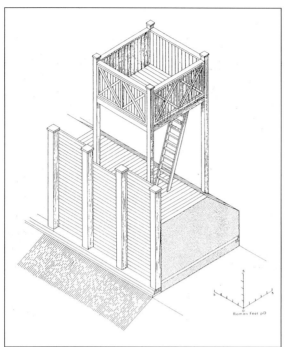

17 *A hypothetical axonometric reconstruction of the defences of the legionary fortress, based on evidence from excavation*

scenario is surely appropriate for the fortress at Wroxeter itself since the new Roman name for the site was *Viroconium*–the settlement of *Virico*. We have no way of knowing who *Virico* was but his name surely suggests he was a local man rather than a soldier. Indeed, it is possible that excavations beneath the later city's market hall (*macellum*) may have found his farm or that of a neighbour since traces of the corner of an enclosure have been found here. More plausibly, perhaps, the name may originally have been applied to the Wrekin itself and could have been transferred to the new settlement. In addition to the slighting of a farmstead, there seems little doubt that the land on which the fortress was built was prime arable land and this too will have been seized. Indeed, nothing would have portrayed more graphically the new regime than the summary acquisition of land in this way for use by the state. The appropriation of land did not just affect the area of the fortress, however. A *cordon sanitaire* was also drawn around it and probably the smaller auxiliary forts too, although obviously to a lesser extent. The purpose of this was not just to keep the native population away but primarily to allow the army room to train and manoeuvre if attacked, and also to provide fodder for the horses and other livestock living in the fort. This type of land was thus known as the *prata legionis*, the legion's meadows.

The establishment of the legionary fortress took place at a date between 52–7, and may have coincided with the push into mid- and north Wales which was undertaken by the governor, Quintus Veranius. As we have seen, the site had natural advantages in terms of the routes in the area but also conformed to the other requirements of an army base: it was close to water, the land was free-draining and not liable to flood, and the area enclosed within the walls was relatively level although defended by natural valleys to the north and south and by the low river cliff to the west. The fortress was probably

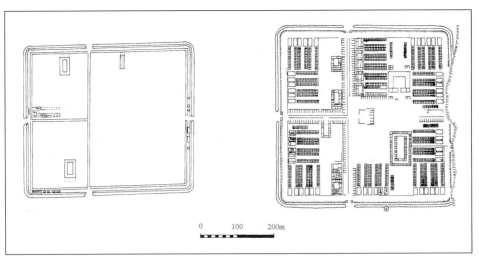

0   100   200m

18 *A comparison of the layouts of the legionary fortresses at Wroxeter and Inchtuthil*

constructed by the *XIIII Gemina* legion, whose previous base had been at Mancetter in Warwickshire (or, less likely, at Leicester). Its layout is imperfectly understood since it lies deeply buried beneath the later city but its boundaries are known on three sides through a combination of excavation and aerial photography. The western defences were located beneath the *macellum* and show most clearly the method of construction (**17**). This involved building a rampart of earth faced with turves, the earth coming from two ditches dug immediately in front of the rampart. The base was constructed on a raft of timbers and at the front of the rampart was a row of horizontal timbers supporting a vertical, planked façade. This timber revetment was tied into the rampart by angled braces and further horizontal timbers buried in it so that movement could be minimised while the earth and turves settled. The back of the rampart was similarly revetted although not to the same height as the front. At the upper level of the rampart, vertical timbers were incorporated into the internal framework to allow the construction of the parapet and, at intervals, more substantial timbers for towers. Only one side of the west gate has been examined and not enough is known to reconstruct its precise form, but since this was the principal gate, the *porta praetoria*, it is likely to have been of dual carriageway width. Above the gates there will have been towers and a fighting platform with, to either side, a ramp (*ascensus*) allowing the garrison to man the walls swiftly if required. For the same reason, there was a broad street, the intervallum road, running behind the rampart around the full circuit of its defences. Of the other sides of the fortress, the north side has been seen only in aerial photographs where it shows as a narrow dark band beneath the later city before turning at the north-east corner to form the east wall (see **11**). The eastern defences have been sectioned in excavation showing that the later city's defences lie directly on top of the slighted legionary defences. The last side, the south, has yet to be discovered but it must lie on or near the modern road known as Patch Lane. The area of about 40 acres (16ha) thus enclosed is rather more square than rectangular. Its nearest parallel is the later fortress of Inchtuthil in Scotland which appears closely to match Wroxeter both in size and in overall layout (**18**).

19 *A photograph of the legionary barrack blocks under excavation. The wall lines show as dark linear patches in the pale natural sand. The dark circular patches represent the remains of posts*

20 *An aerial photograph of the centre of Wroxeter taken in the drought of 1975. North is at the top. The bend of the River Severn can be seen on the extreme left and the sinuous course of the Bell Brook at the top of the photograph. Immediately apparent are the regular street grid and plans of many buildings. Note that some fields have produced relatively poor responses (e.g. the triangular field bottom right). The narrow trenches lying to the north of this field (g) are Stephen Johnson's excavations on the defences. Within the* forum boarium *enclosure (h) is a rectangular building (k) with numerous regularly-spaced posts within it. This is probably a military granary (see **16**). The large house shown in **21** is at (m)*

Of the internal buildings of the fortress, very few have been seen and fewer still excavated. Those that have been confirmed are those found by Dr Graham Webster during his excavations within the area of the town baths. These consisted of the remains of the barrack blocks of which mostly only the foundation trenches survived. These were narrow trenches into which horizontal beams were laid to support prefabricated wall panels (**19**). As is normal, the centurion's quarters take up one end of the barracks with the much smaller rooms of the legionaries beyond. The overall dimensions of the barracks are not known but the size of the rooms of the ordinary soldiers show that life must have been awkward and uncomfortable when the entire force was in camp at any one time.

Also seen in excavation, and to a lesser extent in aerial photographs, are the buildings cut into the back of the ramparts which may have had a variety of functions ranging from store houses to offices for clerks. One of the excavated examples had a fireplace inserted later, suggesting that, for some, life in the garrison was more comfortable. Cut into the back of the rampart elsewhere will have been the soldier's cooking hearths and latrines. Of the other buildings in the fortress, we can only be confident of the existence of an isolated granary seen near the northern defences as a cropmark during the drought summer of 1975 (**20**). Although excavation alone will prove this to be a military granary, it is aligned on the fortress defences and is closely comparable both in size and location to a granary on the west side of the Inchtuthil fortress. Of the headquarters building (*principia*) with its offices, shrine and parade hall, nothing is known, and the same is true of the commandant's house (*praetorium*) and the houses of the tribunes. It is possible to guess at their size and something of their appearance since the Inchtuthil fortress provides some idea of how much land would be allocated to each of these buildings.

Of the remaining buildings, the larger number were for storage and equipment. In many respects a fortress was like a small town and therefore had to be constantly supplied with food and materials to keep it functioning. There will have been several granaries. At Inchtuthil there was space for eight, whose plans are easily distinguished by the forest of posts and external buttresses which supported the floor and took the weight of the foodstuffs pressing against the walls. Other storehouses had extended porches so that wagons could load beneath them without their contents being exposed to the weather. Elsewhere there were doubtless workshops (*fabrica*) where blacksmiths, armourers, farriers, wood- and leather-workers will have plied their trades – in all cases soldiers trained in their chosen craft. There will also have been masons to provide the essential stone-built elements of the fortress, namely those buildings such as baths which had to be directly heated or had open fires in them. In addition to those soldiers trained as craftsmen a substantial number of personnel, involved in administration, had the task of keeping track of the soldiers and ensuring the regular supply of goods and services to the legion. The health and leisure interests of the men would also be catered for through the provision of a large hospital, whose distinctive double-shell plan has yet to be recognised at Wroxeter, and of a bath house. Dr Graham Webster has suggested that the baths may have been built near the headquarters building. Alternatively they could be the unfinished legionary-style baths located outside the west gate, beneath the later forum, which Donald Atkinson excavated in the 1920s.

The occupation of the fortress will have had a profound impact on the surrounding countryside, not least in the provision of adequate food for the garrison. Indeed, the *Cornovii*, uniquely among the tribes of Britain, had to support two legions within their territory, at Chester and Wroxeter, between the 70s and about 90 when the fortress at Wroxeter was finally abandoned. This period in particular must have put an enormous strain on the tribe and its resources. The construction of the fortress itself demanded huge quantities of timber, which was dressed before transport to the site since the usual practice was to prefabricate the buildings as much as possible. The legionary craftsmen will also have been responsible for creating all the necessary metalwork such as nails, hinges, locks, and other furniture which were used in the buildings, the iron probably being locally smelted. The abundant supplies of lead in the region were exploited to produce plumbing and roof coverings while legionary tilers will have constructed kilns

21 *An aerial photograph of the area to the west of the modern farm buildings (see **20**). On the right is a minor road running along the river cliff. Beside it are the pale parchmarks of several large town houses. The largest (m) has a road with narrow ditches to either side, running directly towards it. Another (n) lies partially obscured beneath the corner of an unresponsive field. To the left of the latter are two parallel dark lines (p) which curve to extend beneath the largest building. A road can be seen to cross these ditches showing that the ditches are early, possibly relating to the fortress*

for the production of the many thousands of tiles needed for the roofs of the buildings and for other structures, such as hypocausts. As they were a fire hazard many of these crafts and industries would not have been located within the fortress and so there is likely to have been an annexe containing them, as is seen in many other forts and fortresses throughout the empire.

A possible candidate for such an annexe is the double-ditched enclosure, one side of which runs west from the north-west corner of the fortress enclosing the area up to the river cliff (**21**). The unfinished baths were located within this enclosed area, reinforcing the suggestion that this building belongs to the military phase. Another area possibly under military control lay to the north of the fortress where a substantial ditch and bank are known to have run along the crest of the southern edge of the Bell Brook valley, enclosing a trapezoidal area (see **16**). The excavation of a trench across this feature by Dame Kathleen Kenyon showed that it was created in the first century and it has been

22 *Military tombstones from Wroxeter's fort and fortress. Top left, Tib. Claud. Tirintius, cavalryman of* Eq. Coh. I[?] Thracum; *top right [T] Flaminius,* aquilifer *(eagle-standard bearer) of legio XIIII Gem.; bottom left C. Mannius Secundus,* beneficarius legati praetorii *(clerk to the officer commanding) legio XX; bottom right M. Petronius, soldier of legio XIIII Gem*

suggested by Dr Graham Webster that the enclosed area formed the *canabae* (literally 'the booths') of the fortress which catered for the recreational needs of the soldiers, principally food, drink, and sex. Due to the nature of the transactions being carried on in such areas, they were usually under military control, hence the necessity to defend or at least define the areas but they had to be isolated from the fortress so that discipline would not be affected more than absolutely necessary.

At some distance away, and probably to the south so as to be near the ford, may have been the civilian settlement (*vicus*, or market) which gradually grew up as locals were attracted to the spending power of the soldiers. Here could be found the common-law wives and children of the soldiers who, although not officially permitted to marry, could form unofficial liaisons whose resulting children could be retrospectively recognised after the retirement of the soldiers, an important benefit for the wives and children since it would automatically confirm citizenship on them too. Also located in the *vicus* would be other citizens and locals who had a vested interest in being close to the army, such as traders, or craftsmen, such as potters. The latter can be traced through the survival of their products, albeit in a fragmentary condition, and these provide insights into trading patterns and the origins of the potters themselves. There will also have been suppliers of brooches and other fine metalwork as well as all the other types of artefacts that soldiers and their families might spend money on. There is little doubt that the *vicus* was also where some soldiers who had received their honourable discharge went to live so that they could continue to be involved in army life, albeit peripherally, and take advantage of the offer of land as part of their discharge entitlement. A number of tombstones found in Wroxeter attest such men (**22**). From *legio XIIII Gemina* we know of Titus Flaminius from Faventia who was an eagle bearer (*aquilifer*) in his legion, Marcus Petronius from Vicetia, and an unknown man from Lyons. The first two of these died whilst still in service, Flaminius after 22 years and Petronius after 18. The other soldier known from Wroxeter, Gaius Mannius Secundus from Pollentia, was a clerk (*beneficarius*) to the legate in command of *legio XX* and had died after 31 years' service. Also recorded is Placida, perhaps one of the soldier's wives, who had died at 55, and Deuccus who must be a relative since they are commemorated on the same tombstone.

It is unclear whether it was the army which encouraged people to settle near the fortress to supply the army's needs, or whether people gravitated towards it anyway: probably it was a mixture of both causes. Certainly, it is true to say that there can have been no simple link between the presence of the troops and the establishment and growth of the civilian settlement since it is apparent that over the 30-year life of the fortress, the number of troops fluctuated widely and the status of the fortress was gradually diminished.

Undoubtedly, the period between its foundation in the mid-50s until the beginning of the campaigns of Agricola in the late 70s saw the main flowering of the fortress, with first *legio XIIII Gemina* and then, after 60, *legio XX* supplying the garrison. For much of this period in the late 50s–60 and again in 74–7, the legions were dealing with the conquest of central and north Wales. In between, they were dealing with the Boudican revolt and its aftermath in 60, and undertaking the conquest of *Brigantia* from about 71. Thus, Wroxeter must have been well behind the front line, only coming into its own as a base during the winter months. After the commencement of Agricola's campaigns in northern Britain in about 78, *legio XX* will have moved further and further away until its lines of communication with its notional base at Wroxeter became untenable. According to Dr Graham Webster, it was during this campaign that the fortress was effectively downgraded, its defences being slighted and some of the buildings abandoned. There may have been a skeleton administration in residence until they too joined their legion at its new base at Inchtuthil in Scotland.

For a decade or so the legion must have moved to and fro between these two bases while Agricola's campaign ground on in northern Britain until the Emperor Domitian called it to a halt and ordered a partial withdrawal leading to the abandonment of Inchtuthil in about 86–7, before it had even been finished. The legion may well have returned to Wroxeter, putting the base back into some sort of order and perhaps starting to build a new bath house, but before the work could be completed, the Emperor's fresh campaigns on the continent demanded that one of the four legions of Britain be withdrawn. The legion chosen was the *II Adiutrix* which had been based at Chester since the end of the 70s, which meant that the *XX*, now styled *Valeria Victrix*, had to leave Wroxeter to take over the fortress at Chester, a far more logical base for holding northern Wales and Britain. It was destined to remain there for at least the next 250 years. Thus, by the beginning of the 90s Wroxeter's fortress had ceased to exist, its defences being thrown down and the less adaptable of its buildings being demolished. Presumably, although we have no evidence for what happened next, it seems likely that at this point military control over much of Cornovian territory ceased and the land around Wroxeter, with the exception of that parcelled out for retired soldiers, was passed back into tribal ownership and administration. The civil governor of Britain, based in London, will no doubt have instructed and helped the tribe to establish the new order, but effectively the fledgling city was left to its own devices.

3 The impact of Rome

As we have seen, the arrival of Rome in Cornovian territory set in train a series of changes that must have profoundly affected Cornovian society. If the Iron Age people of the area may be characterised archaeologically as being materially restricted, then the Roman army by contrast was the consumer society *par excellence*. The army expected, and got, a Mediterranean diet in the north-European world – olive oil, wine and fish-sauce (*garum* or *liquamen*) were transported across hundreds of miles to the legions stationed in foreign parts. With these goods, presumably procured under contracts from suppliers, came fashionable pottery, glass, and metalwork, the more archaeologically-obvious commodities, and many others such as fabrics, papyrus, and more exotic foodstuffs which archaeologists rarely recover. Not all goods came by this tortuous route, however. As much as possible was acquired locally and since the army did not wish to alienate the native population more than necessary it is likely that a system for payment for such goods will have been established. The army's requirements for grain, fodder, meat, dairy products, fruit and vegetables, leather, wood for fuel and building, drink and pottery, to list the more obvious items, will have been constant although the precise quantities will have varied according to the season and the numbers stationed in the forts and fortresses of the region.

It is easy to imagine the impact of these demands on the local society. There had always been grain surpluses whose presence is attested by the numerous storage buildings found in the hillforts of the region, but any surplus was largely for use as seed and there will have been a limited amount for disposal elsewhere. If the Roman army wished to buy large quantities of grain from the tribe, then either agricultural production must have been rapidly and substantially improved, or the local population will have gone without to feed the soldiers. Almost certainly there will have been a larger surplus in cattle, and possibly to a lesser extent in horses and sheep, since not only may wealth have been measured in the number of animals one owned but also the region has its richest agricultural potential in pasture. To the Roman army agricultural surpluses must have been extremely attractive and it cannot have taken long for the tribal aristocracy and the rest of the local population to realise that there were considerable profits to be made from supplying the army with the necessities of life.

The notion of profit in itself of course was a profound change. Before the arrival of Rome, wealth may not have been measured personally but may rather have been perceived as tribal property. This did not accord with Roman law, under which the *Cornovii* now had to operate, and it may be that those who controlled the tribe's wealth suddenly found themselves in possession of a windfall as the mutually-owned wealth of the tribe was converted overnight into private fortunes. It is unlikely that the lower-status Cornovian had much to say in these developments, although of course small-scale landowners who produced an agricultural surplus on their farms might sell directly outside the tribe for the first time rather than being required to put their produce into communal stores. Those who did take their surplus products to the army will have immediately encountered something else novel: money. Although one or two high value Iron Age coins are known from the territory (mostly those of the *Dobunni*, in addition to those already mentioned from Meols), there is no evidence that the *Cornovii* were a coin-using society and certainly were not coin-producers. The few specimens that are known were possibly exchanged as gifts or were prestige items for display rather than use. With the arrival of Rome all of this will have changed. Suddenly wealth was measured in terms of discs of metal rather than heads of cattle, although in practice the full introduction of coinage into native society may have been quite slow.

However, it is unlikely that the *Cornovii* had remained ignorant of money before their conquest. There had no doubt been dealings with tribes who used money and even if money had only been observed in use, the principles were surely known. Nonetheless there must have been a period of adjustment while people got used to the concept and the transition cannot have happened without some having their fingers burnt. The Romans too were aware of the lack of Cornovian skill in money matters and some will have taken advantage of it. Reading Tacitus' account of the Boudican revolt leaves one in little doubt that unscrupulous money lenders, the great philosopher Seneca among them, had reduced the Icenian aristocracy to the desperate measure of revolt by calling in their loans, on the back of exorbitant rates of interest, after the death of Prasutagus.

Of course, other opportunities will have been presented by the arrival of the army. The most obvious is that local men could now enlist for service in the *auxilia*, the non-citizen branch of the army. This would bring considerable benefits including regular pay, the possibility of social advancement, and most important of all the prospect of citizenship on discharge. Recruits would, however, have to face up to the fact that enlistment meant service elsewhere in the empire, not in Britain. Women too might be directly affected by the army – we know of at least one Cornovian woman, whose tombstone was found at the fort at Ilkley in Yorkshire, who may have been married to a soldier or perhaps a trader.

For most inhabitants, however, the greatest opportunities lay in the provision of goods and services. The demands for wood for fuel and for construction will have mostly been met by the army itself sending out foraging parties, but there may well have been a market for woodworkers to exploit. We know that the *Cornovii* were capable of producing fine lathe-turned bowls, for example those found at the Breiddin hillfort, and these will no doubt have been in demand at the fortress. Similarly, there must have been leather-workers and tanners who could have found a ready employment in the *canabae* or annexe of the fort if there was a shortage of skilled personnel for such work. Inevitably, these local people will soon have picked up Roman working practices and techniques, thus starting the process of assimilation generally called Romanization. This must also have been a boom period for metalworkers. The Celts had always been

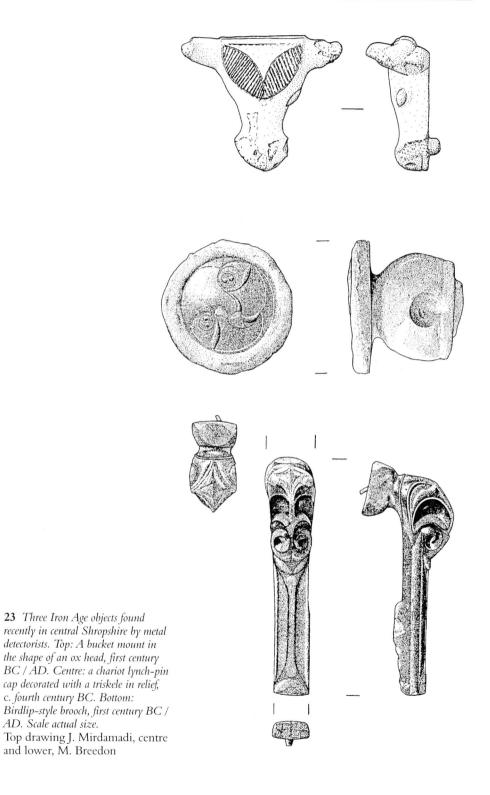

23 *Three Iron Age objects found recently in central Shropshire by metal detectorists. Top: A bucket mount in the shape of an ox head, first century BC / AD. Centre: a chariot lynch-pin cap decorated with a triskele in relief, c. fourth century BC. Bottom: Birdlip-style brooch, first century BC / AD. Scale actual size.*
Top drawing J. Mirdamadi, centre and lower, M. Breedon

24 *An iron die with incised Celtic-style patterns on two faces which was found on the forum site in the 1920s. It was used by metalworkers to emboss sheet metal. Scale in cm*

renowned for their exceptional skills in iron smithing and in bronze founding and, although the evidence for Cornovian metalwork is scanty, there seems little doubt that they produced good-quality metalwork, as is increasingly being recognised from the finds made by metal detectorists in Shropshire and Cheshire (**23**). These local smiths will have continued to make their domestic products such as plough shares and other iron tools but the manufacture of weapons of war and the trappings associated with warfare, such as chariots, will have been outlawed by the Romans who did not allow natives to carry arms. Their skills will not have gone to waste, however, since there was a ready market for fine metalwork particularly among the army whose soldiers had to purchase their own equipment and its embellishment was a matter for personal choice. The Celts' love of enamelled bronze and repoussé plates proved very popular and especially so with the auxiliary troops, many of whom were themselves from Celtic areas. Direct evidence for these metalworking skills has been found in the waste castings for brooches, spoons and other items and in the discovery of an iron die for repoussé work found in other excavations in the city centre (**24**). There is also evidence for metalworking hearths in the immediate vicinity of Wroxeter derived from fieldwalking and from the results of the geophysical survey of the enclosed area of the city.

There were also new skills to acquire, such as throwing pots on a wheel. The archaeological evidence shows that the potters arrived with the army since the shapes of the pots, and some of the names of the potters stamped onto their products, can be traced to other areas of Britain and even the continent. From the second century, the bulk of the locally-produced pottery is a red or, occasionally, grey ware known as 'Severn Valley ware' which can be found along the whole length of Welsh borderlands. There seems little doubt that this pottery derives from a late Iron Age tradition found in the heartland of the *Dobunni*, which seems to have found a ready, and huge, market with the arrival of the Roman army when Gloucester, Cirencester and other forts were constructed. These Dobunnic potters then seem to have followed the army into Cornovian territory where the distinctive styles and shapes of their pottery, which have close links with leather and wooden forms and imitate the sort of decoration of such vessels, will have found a ready market among the natives and Romans. The potters also added many forms which catered for distinctly Roman tastes too, such as flagons and lamps. For the more specialised wares, such as the heavy, gritted mixing bowls (*mortaria*) ubiquitous in Roman kitchens, the army had to rely on specialist potters who appear to have followed the army to supply their needs. In the case of Wroxeter, the locally-produced *mortaria* find echoes in the products of the kilns in *Rhaetia* (modern-day Austria and Switzerland) although in time, of course, local labour would have been trained to produce such wares.

An even more exotic trade is hinted at from an excavation opposite the present church of St Andrew in Wroxeter village. Here, evidence for a roadside glassworks was found, including considerable quantities of glass waste and scrap glass (cullet) for reuse, associated with an annealing hearth and crucibles. The early date of this complex suggests that it was linked either to the fortress or the early city. It is probable that rather than making glass vessels here, those working the recycled glass were making glass beads and bangles, a trade linked with enamelling and one with which the Celts were already familiar, as is attested by finds of Iron Age beads within the vicinity of Wroxeter and in Cornovian territory generally. Other trades which are less prominent in the

25 *A number of deep pits, interlinked by a two-phase timber-lined gully (a, b), excavated on Site A, baths basilica. It was thought that these pits may have been used for tanning or fulling, perhaps in association with buildings found adjacent (see 10)*

archaeological record must have been equally important, for example cloth and leather production. In the medieval period Shropshire, and the towns of Ludlow and Shrewsbury in particular, were renowned for their production of high-quality wool, and the leather industry was a notable force in many of the Shropshire towns. The products of these industries rarely survive at Wroxeter but there is evidence for their production in the numerous spindle whorls and the inter-linked pits for tanning or fulling which have been found on numerous sites in the city, even within the precinct of the public baths complex itself (**25**).

Although these trades will inevitably have been reliant on the army for their contracts, there seems little doubt that even after the army moved on there will have been a market for these goods from the steadily growing population of the city. Direct archaeological evidence of this is rare at Wroxeter since so little of the early city has been excavated or recognised but there is evidence from the strip-buildings fronting Watling Street, excavated by J.P. Bushe-Fox, that there were a number of artisans in the city whose trades seem to have been plied after the army's departure (**26**). It must be assumed that goods were being sold to the citizens in these shops or in the markets so that whoever was visiting the city would have the opportunity to buy them. There may also have been a certain amount of scope for the peddling of products in the hinterland of Wroxeter.

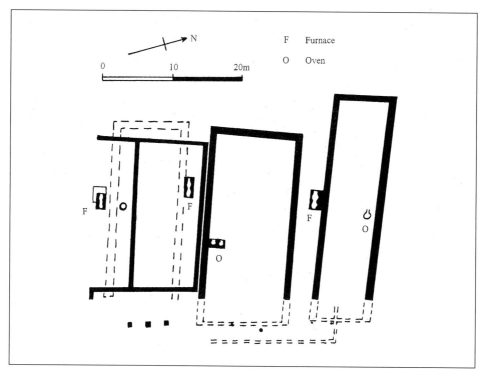

26 *Early strip-buildings excavated by Bushe-Fox. Note the small furnaces, ovens and the apparently open façades suggesting that these were workshops as well, or perhaps rather than, houses*

Brooch makers, for example, might well have set out from their workshops in Wroxeter with a stock of cast blanks which they could then work up elsewhere to the client's taste with a readily-constructed furnace or hearth with a field anvil.

Stone masons too will have been able to ply their trade after the army's withdrawal. During the life of the legionary fortress, trained masons would have been fully occupied both in providing the basic ashlar building stone and lathe-turned columns that many of the buildings required, and will also have created the decorative carvings, such as column capitals, that were essential for the embellishment of any classical-style building. In times when no building was under construction, such men would be usefully employed in carving tombstones or statues, such as the lovely water-nymph found beneath the *macellum* which must originally have come from a fountain within the fortress (**27**). Later, the building boom created by the foundation of the new city will have supplied plenty of work for stone masons and their associates in other building trades, such as plasterers, painters and mosaicists. That such craftsmen were ultimately trained in the legions can be demonstrated from the decorative details found on stone capitals in particular which show links with those carved on the Rhineland, precisely the area that the legions who occupied Britain had been drawn from.

In addition to fostering trade and industry, the army during its period at Wroxeter swiftly developed those extractive industries which had hardly begun to be exploited by the Iron Age tribe (**28**). Primary among these industries will have been the mining and

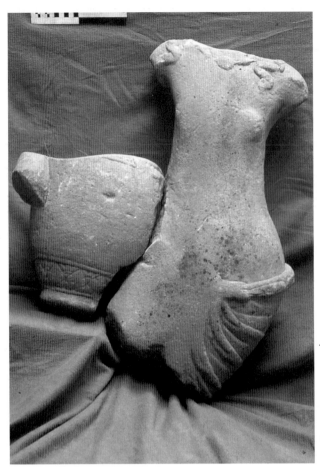

27 *The Wroxeter Nymph and her Jar, found beneath the* macellum. *This statue may originally have been located in the legionary headquarters or commander's building. Later, it was reused with the result that the torso was worn away in places. The detailing of palmettes and concentric rings on the water jar shows that it was modelled on a metal prototype*

processing of lead from the western hills of Shropshire and, to a lesser extent, in Cheshire, and the identification and exploitation of stone for the building industry. As discussed in chapter 2, salt and copper had been exploited heavily in prehistory and here the Roman army merely took over existing industries. In the case of salt, a state monopoly, the army will have taken direct control, as is evidenced by the forts placed at Middlewich, Nantwich and Northwich in Cheshire. The local producers of salt may still have been allowed to continue their work but their products will have been taken by the state and there remains the possibility that the army exploited the resource itself. After the mid-second century, salt manufacture appears to have been farmed out as concessions to local entrepreneurs who, in return for a payment, were allowed to produce the salt themselves, extracting their profit as they did so. The names of some of these individuals, invariably Celtic, are known from the lead salt pans which have occasionally been discovered in the region.

Copper mining was not an imperial monopoly and the most extensive mine in the area, within the hillfort at Llanymynech near Oswestry, presumably continued under local, and probably tribal, ownership and use. Certainly there is no known Roman fort nearby to indicate imperial interest in the mine and its profits. The hill itself also

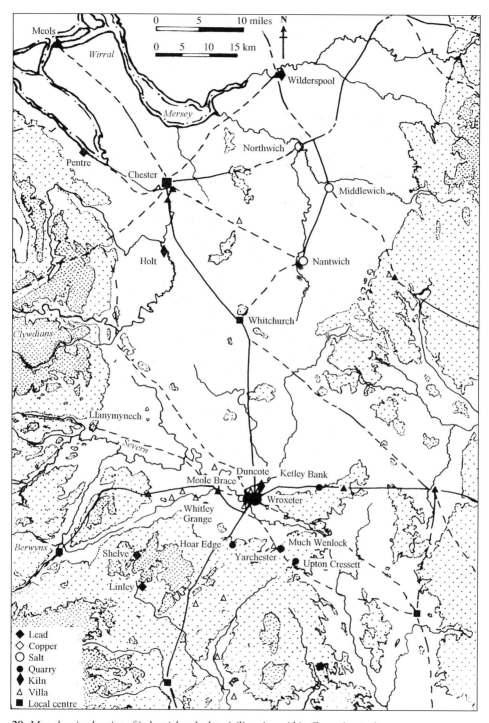

28 *Map showing location of industrial and other civilian sites within Cornovian territory*

29 *An aerial photograph of the water channels at Linley left by the process of 'hushing' (i.e. washing away topsoil to expose ore-bearing veins). The channels show as faint, roughly parallel lines running from left to right*

attracted the interest of the Roman masons since the copper veins occur within a very fine-grained porcellaneous limestone which proved to be an excellent source for the white tesserae used in mosaics both in Wroxeter and in the more elaborately-decorated villas surrounding the city.

Other sources of stone were also probably initially identified and exploited by the military since their engineers will have needed to construct some of the fortress buildings in stone from the outset. Not surprisingly, most of the stone quarries seem to have been located on or near the newly-created roads since it was here that the army surveyors will have exposed and seen the bedrock. Two principal freestone types are known at Wroxeter: a red or purple sandstone known as Keele Beds, and two grades of buff or yellow sandstone known as Hoar Edge Grit. The red sandstone has been linked with a quarry at Ketley Bank in modern-day Telford, some 8 miles (13km) east of Wroxeter, which lies on the line of Watling Street, but other more local sources are possible since this sandstone outcrops throughout the region. Hoar Edge is a scarp, like its more famous neighbour Wenlock Edge, lying 6 miles (10km) to the south of Wroxeter, which produces a coarse and rather friable stone suitable for larger blocks, and a finer yellow stone suitable for carving – practically all the known inscriptions from the city are in this finer stone. Again, the quarry lies close to the Roman road, in this instance the road leading south-west from Wroxeter. Another road to the south-east provided limestone essential for the production of mortar and plaster from the extensive outcrops at Much Wenlock, about 7 miles (11km) from the city. The same road probably also supplied micaceous flagstone for roofing slates, probably from quarries in the vicinity of a major unenclosed site at Upton Cressett near Bridgnorth which lies 12 miles (20km) from Wroxeter. There also seems to be some evidence for the small-scale use of coal since pieces have been found in excavations at Wroxeter, but the preferred alternative for fuel was coppice wood.

The last of the major mining resources to be exploited was lead, which outcrops at Linley, Shelve, and Snailbeach in south-west Shropshire. Although a certain amount of lead was used by the Iron Age metalsmiths, especially as a constituent of bronze to make it flow more readily into moulds, the main period of exploitation belongs in the Roman period and was almost certainly initiated by the military. This was not only because lead was used extensively by the army's engineers in buildings and to a lesser extent by the armourers and other metalworkers in the fortress but primarily because the ore was silver-bearing so that if smelted in a cuppelation furnace, a by-product of the lead would have been silver. Naturally, all bullion mines were under the control of the state since the basis of the Roman economy was the use of gold and silver coinage. The mines were thus protected by the army which built small forts, such as that at Linley Hill for example, with slaves or criminals supplying the labour in the mines. The extraction and processing of the ore was effected using two methods: drift mines and 'hushing'. The latter method involved washing away the thin topsoil over the rock to expose the ore-bearing veins which could then be mined conventionally. The remains of the reservoirs and channels resulting from this process may still be seen at Linley Hall (**29**) and excavations in the mid-nineteenth century appear to have found the remains of the complex of buildings associated with the processing of the ore.

A similar complex is known from Pentre, Flintshire, in the territory of the neighbouring tribe, the *Deceangli*. There, evidence of the processing buildings and associated accommodation have recently been excavated. As with the salt industry, by the mid-second century or even during the late first century, the lead industry seems to have been farmed out to lessees, as evidenced by the pigs bearing the Emperor Hadrian's name with the names of those running the concession from the mines at Snailbeach and Snead, and on a stray find from Aston near Bishop's Castle. The production of the lead mines seems to have been used largely within the vicinity of Wroxeter itself and it is certainly true that all the ingots found in the northern part of Cornovian territory, at Chester and Runcorn for example, carry the label *Decang.* to show that they originated in the tribal area of the *Deceangli*. This would seem a suitably pragmatic approach to supplying such a heavy material to where it was required and for similar reasons the lead pans found at Northwich and Nantwich may be derived from Derbyshire lead rather than from the mines in Shropshire or Flintshire.

It might be anticipated that the eventual withdrawal of the army from the Wroxeter region will have had a profound effect on trade. However, there does not seem to have been a fall-off in goods arriving at Wroxeter since there is a barely perceptible change in the quantity of goods supplied after the army departed, although some of the finest pottery wares, such as the delicate Lyons Ware beakers, no longer seem to be imported to the city. Instead, the local pottery industry appears to have continued to produce an extensive range of table and kitchen wares from the local clays, their production being supplemented by the continued import of the more common tablewares, such as the products of more distant kilns in Britain, and of samian ware.

As yet, only two definite pottery kiln sites have been excavated at Wroxeter. One lay outside the north-west gate and has never been adequately published but seems to have produced the Rhaetian-style *mortaria* found commonly within the city. This kiln can be dated to the mid-second century and must therefore relate to the city rather than the fortress. Another kiln was excavated by the late Dr John Houghton after it had been seen eroding at the confluence of the Tern and Severn at Attingham Park, about half a mile (1km) from Wroxeter. The pottery here was of classic Severn Valley type although the date of the kiln seems to have been third century. Another kiln is suggested about two miles (2km) further out from Wroxeter at Duncote Farm where excavations found a substantial group of mis-fired pottery (wasters) in the ditch of a farmstead, although the kilns themselves were not located. In earlier excavations wasters have been found at Wroxeter itself and these prove conclusively that the industry was operating within and around the city.

Despite the substantial nature of local pottery production, there was also a strong trade in both provincial and imported wares. Notable among the early provincial wares are large groups of white clay *mortaria* which came from Mancetter-Hartshill in Warwickshire. This region may lie within Cornovian territory, but this is by no means certain. More likely, in common with other major pottery industries in Britain, production could have been situated on the border of two tribal territories to exploit both and perhaps evade tribal tolls and obligations. Also imported in substantial quantities in this early period were wares from *Verulamium* (St Albans), and 'Black Burnished Ware' from Dorset. Indeed, this latter ware continued to feature in Wroxeter's pottery market throughout the Roman period until it ceased production early in the fifth century. Of the wares imported from the continent, the most important in the early period was samian ware which came from kilns in Gaul. The most

30 *The forum gutter find as discovered in 1923. The top photograph shows several large mortarium mixing bowls lying where they fell. That below shows nests of plain samian dishes (1-4) with, in the foreground, the unused Kentish ragstone whetstones (see **colour plate 4**). It is thought that the bowls, dishes and whetstones were set on stalls sheltered by the colonnade, one of whose columns is at 5, and that when the forum burnt down, these stalls were upset into the gutter*

significant number came from the Central Gaulish kilns but earlier examples from Southern Gaul or Northern Italy, and later examples from Eastern Gaul, have also been found in the city. In this Wroxeter is entirely typical. The huge scale of production of samian ware meant that virtually every Roman site in Britain produces sherds, and it even appears regularly in sites beyond the frontiers of the Empire. Also imported from the same source, although in lesser quantities, are the fine wares from the kilns of Central Gaul, such as Lezoux, which were producing delicate beakers which often imitated metal vessels.

Both samian and Mancetter-Hartshill *mortaria* were represented in the famous Wroxeter gutter find made in 1923 when Donald Atkinson uncovered stacks of unused vessels which had fallen into the gutter when the forum caught fire between 165–75 (**30**). Quite why these pieces were never recovered is not clear since they were mostly unbroken but the way that they had fallen suggests that they had probably been standing on trader's stalls waiting to be sold. Another of the gutter finds, a consignment of Kentish ragstone whetstones, had perhaps been added to the samian group when the pottery had been landed in London, the *mortaria* being added en route via Watling Street (**colour plate 4**).

Other imports can also be identified from even further afield, such as the storage containers (*amphorae*) carrying olive oil from *Baetica* (south-western Spain) in the distinctive globular *amphorae* known as Dressel 20. Initially, these vessels had been imported for the benefit of the military who will have been used to using olive oil in cooking and although it is conceivable that the native population adopted Mediterranean eating habits as enthusiastically as is the case in modern Britain, it seems equally possible that the continuing supply of olive oil may have been for use in the public baths where it was an essential element of Roman bathing, and for use in domestic lamps. Wine too travelled in *amphorae* and certainly reached Wroxeter where it was used as an alternative to the native drink, Celtic beer. By the third and fourth centuries, however, it is likely that the wine imports were weighted heavily in favour of the vineyards of the Rhineland and Mosel, a trade that is more difficult to prove since the numerous carved stone monuments of Germany make it clear that the wine was exported in wooden barrels rather than in pottery containers. The trade is attested rather by other Rhenish imports which no doubt arrived in smaller quantities but which have survived in the archaeological record, namely glass vessels, fine-ware pottery beakers and lava mill- or quern-stones.

The transport of all these goods to Wroxeter was either by the road system or by the River Severn. Despite the numerous advantages in terms of cost, the Severn seems to have been a neglected route since wherever it is possible to judge how goods arrived at Wroxeter, it seems clear that they came by road rather than the river. This is true even of such heavy materials as stone. It is possible that this came about because, if material were being taken by road under an army or other contract, the cost would be carried by those responsible for the contract. The supplier might then feel free to load more than required by the contract and sell the surplus en route. Alternatively, there may have been a sufficiently large market at Wroxeter to make the effort of transporting material there worthwhile. One other possible stimulus for the trade, however, could have been that the goods were brought back to Wroxeter by traders who were marketing products or raw materials from the territory of the *Cornovii*. If, for example, as suggested earlier, the

1 *A watercolour of the north side of the Old Work, painted by Thomas Girtin in 1798. He has romanticised the subject by adding a few shrubs and a pond in the foreground but the view of the countryside beyond is little changed today*

2 *A watercolour of the north side of the Old Work, painted by Revd Williams, vicar of Battlefield Church, Shrewsbury, in 1788. This view shows the true state of the Old Work with a ploughed field in the foreground. A view of the south side painted by the same artist shows a setting not dissimilar to the foreground in Girtin's watercolour, suggesting that Girtin transposed the more attractive, Romantic, setting from the south side of the Old Work to the north side*

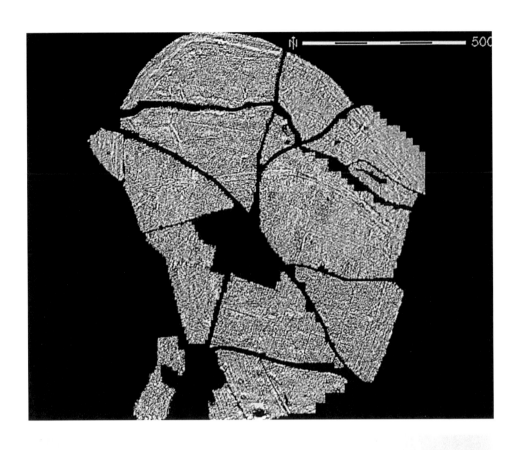

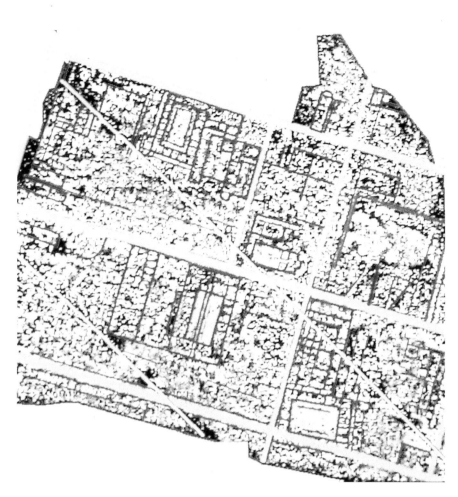

3 *(opposite above) A gradiometry plot of the entire city. At the scale reproduced, much of the detail is inevitably lost but what is apparent is the sheer density of occupation (shown as speckly areas) in contrast to those areas which have little human activity in them (e.g. in the south of the city)*

4 *(opposite below) A selection of whetstones, samian, and mortaria from the forum gutter find*

5 *(above) An interpretation of the gradiometry data south of the baths (see **3**). Two modern pipe trenches have been highlighted in yellow while the Roman street grid is in beige. The walls of the 'church', two courtyard houses, and the* mansio *(bottom right) have been highlighted in red with their internal courtyards in pink*

6 *A reconstructed aerial view by Ivan Lapper of the baths and forum as first built. The dominance of these buildings in the city centre is apparent. They would also have been visible from miles away in the surrounding countryside*

7 *A view by Ivan Lapper of the exercise yard (palaestra) of the baths as first built, in about 150. To the left is the outdoor pool (natatio) whilst to the right is the large exercise hall (baths basilica). Joining the two is a portico*

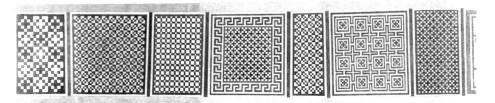

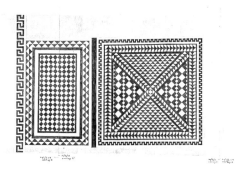

8 *The mosaics of the north aisle of the baths
basilica as reconstructed by Heather Bird from
on-site evidence. There is evidence for patching
and repairs on two separate occasions indicating
that the building was heavily used. In time a
5m (16ft) gap opened up separating the panels
above from those to the right*

9 *A reconstruction of the fragments of ceiling plaster found in the* frigidarium *of the baths. The pattern is
meant to represent the panels of a coffered ceiling*

10 *The gates of St Andrew's church, Wroxeter which were put up in 1868. The square-cut bases came from beneath the sunken-floored barn near the modern museum, as did the capitals, while the shafts may have come from the baths basilica*

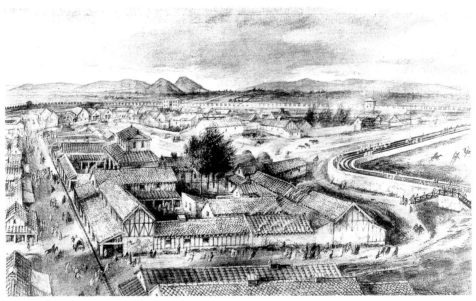

11 *A reconstruction by Alan Sorrell of the south-western part of the city showing the elaborate enclosure behind the temple being used for horse riding (see 42). The temple is the tall building within the courtyard*

WP80 G34 E206

12 *A detail of the roadside water fountain under excavation on the baths basilica site. This feature consisted of a wooden tank, with an overflow to one side, and hollow wooden pipes bringing in water under pressure. It is a testament to the high standards of engineering found in Roman cities*

13 *The tombstone of Cunorix which was ploughed up on the city ramparts in the late 1960s*

14 *A detail from the gradiometry plot (see colour plates 3 and 5) showing the plan of the 'church' and several views from the virtual reality reconstruction of it by Sally Exon*

15 *A watercolour by Steve Cosh of the mosaic found in Wroxeter village in 1827*

16 *A watercolour by David Neal of the Whitley Grange mosaic*

17 *A view along the south aisle of the baths basilica showing the herringbone tile floor laid there after the later third century*

18 *The Wroxeter mirror. Found by Atkinson in the ruins of the forum, it is certainly the most lavish Roman mirror ever found in Britain*

19 *A panel from the coffered ceiling of the Constantinian palace at Trier showing a woman using a silver mirror like that found at Wroxeter. The woman is thought to be either Constantine's wife or sister*

20 *A view of the north portico of the baths basilica showing the faint parallel lines left by the joists of a boardwalk*

21 *The evidence for the façade of Building 7 (see **62**). The two large stones supported a porch, the door posts resting within the shallow square holes behind. On either side of these holes are clay foundations peppered with the holes left by the timber reinforcement of the clay walls*

22 *An aerial view of the Berth at Baschurch, an Iron Age fort located within a low-lying marshy area north-west of Shrewsbury. The site may have been re-occupied in the sub-Roman period and could even be Pengwern, the site of Cynddylan's hall*

23 *The skeleton of a man buried on the baths basilica site between 600 and 790. He lies without grave goods on a north-south alignment*

CM

24 *A gilded bronze Anglo-Saxon strap tag of late ninth century date found in a robbing trench on the baths basilica site. It testifies to the active robbing of the site in the early medieval period*

25a *(and overleaf) Anglo-Saxon carvings of late eighth or early ninth century date built into the south wall of St Andrew's church (a and b) and into the foot of the chancel arch (c). As an eighteenth century engraving shows (70), these objects were once part of a free-standing cross in the churchyard*

25b

25c

wealth of the tribe lay in the production of cloth, raw wool and leather in large quantities, the export of this will have required the use of road or river transport to take the goods out of the territory. Since the wagons and boats would have to return to Wroxeter, they would almost certainly have then been laden with goods on their return journey. Such a mechanism would by-pass the cost of transport since this would presumably be added to the cost of the commodities being exported from the territory.

Once goods arrived at Wroxeter, it is likely that most were consumed within the city, although there does seem to have been a certain amount of redistribution to the immediate vicinity of Wroxeter. The classic example of this comes from the unenclosed roadside settlement at Meole Brace, about 4 miles (6km) west of Wroxeter, where a minor road junction encouraged a small-scale settlement to flourish. The finds from the site showed an unusual pattern with an emphasis on *amphorae*, storage jars, and a larger than average number of keys and weights, leading the excavators to conclude that the site may have been a small market for those who found travel to Wroxeter too far for them. Similar markets are known to have existed outside the long-lived Roman forts of the region, at Whitchurch, Leintwardine and Caersws. Strangely, fieldwork seems to show that little of this material is otherwise making its way to the farms in the countryside around Wroxeter. This may perhaps be a reflection of the continued resistance of the *Cornovii* to consumer goods, a trait traceable within the Iron Age.

The lack of artefacts on excavated rural sites in Shropshire makes their identification and dating difficult, and this in turn obscures how the landscape around Wroxeter was altered first around the fortress and then the city. We have seen that the landscape into which the Roman army moved was one that had already been largely transformed from its natural state into farmsteads, fields, and woodlands. It is clear from our present archaeological knowledge of the Iron Age that in the lowlands at least the population was living in isolated farmsteads rather than collections of houses representing villages. Each farmstead, however, may well have been inhabited by more than one family since it is known that kinship groups rather than the more narrowly defined nuclear families were important among the Celts. Thus at the large triple ditched enclosure at Collfryn in Powys, for example, there is evidence that at least two roundhouses were standing at any one time, suggesting two linked family groups. Such farmsteads will have been largely self-sufficient with perhaps a proportion of the agricultural surplus being rendered to the nearest hillfort in tribute and as allegiance to the larger tribe. This delicate mechanism of self-sufficiency and tribal tithes was wrecked by the arrival of the Roman army and with it the demands of the Roman state through the provincial administration. In some respects, the system will not have changed: tribute was still demanded but, in addition, there was a radical change in the creation of a large, static non-agricultural population whose mere existence demanded a reordering of the landscape to support it.

Of course, even in Iron Age societies there had been 'idle mouths' to feed; for example, the aristocracy and priests will have existed on the tribute and tithes paid into the communal stores, but this was as nothing to compare with the huge demands made by the army and latterly the population of the city. The 5500 men stationed in the fortress of Wroxeter were supplied with rations organised by the commissariat of the legion which will have purchased some supplies brought from a long distance, such as the rations of olive oil and wine already discussed, but will have had to find fresh meat and

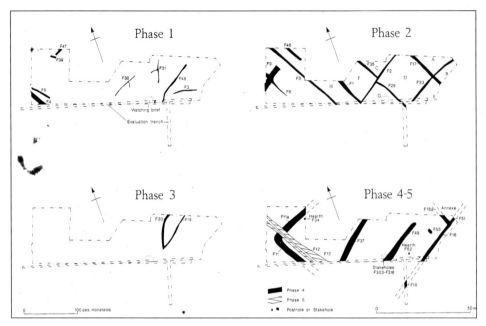

31 *Plans of the features excavated at Duncote Farm. Phase 1 shows scattered Iron Age ditches, probably the remains of a field system. Phase 2 demonstrates the evidence for an early Roman reorganisation of the fields into small-scale plots, perhaps for market gardening. These were largely filled in for phase 3. Finally, in phases 4-5, a square or rectangular enclosure was laid out within which was evidence for industrial activity*

vegetables locally. The discovery of the *Vindolanda* tablets, although of a slightly later date and for a much smaller garrison, have, for the first time, thrown a vivid light onto the process. Some of the documents list in detail the measures of grain, beer, pork, and other commodities required by the troops. The small quantities suggest the sale of these goods by individuals and this must imply local farmers who were exploiting the market. There is no reason why Wroxeter's fortress should not have seen similar trade, albeit on a much larger scale. This may have caused those farmers living close to the fortress to change their farming regime to produce crops such as fresh vegetables and salads rather than grain. This will only have affected those closest to the fortress or, later, the city, since to supply fresh vegetables one would have to live within one day's return journey from the settlement, in other words a radius of a few miles, depending upon access to roads.

The clearest archaeological evidence for this sort of change in the landscape within Wroxeter's hinterland is the complex sequence of alterations to the field system around the settlement at Duncote Farm, about 1 mile (2km) north of Wroxeter. Here, in advance of road construction, excavators identified five phases of activity on a farmstead. The first phase was late Iron Age in date and consisted of an irregular series of ditches which was taken to represent a fragmentary pattern of fields. This was then replaced by an organised chequerboard pattern of small fields laid out within a framework of plots conforming to the Roman acre (**31**). This reorganisation dated to the early second century and was later filled in to be replaced with a less well-ordered system. By the later Roman period, the farm was enclosed within a sub-divided single-ditched compound

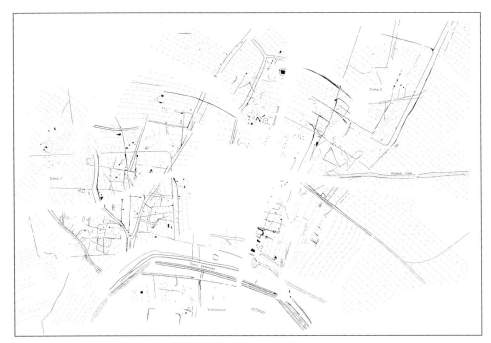

32 *A plan of the mass of cropmarks observed in the northern part of Wroxeter. These represent features of varying dates but a number of elements can be identified. For example, the medieval ridge-and-furrow ploughing marks (plotted here as broken lines) are visible over large areas inside and outside the city defences. Also inside the defences are the possible remains of market garden plots and pits (not all of which have been plotted) and a road. Two camps belonging to the military phase of Wroxeter's life have been singled out from the cropmarks. On the side closest to the city defences in Camp 1 can be seen two roughly rectangular enclosures filled with regular black 'pits' which may be enclosed cemeteries with graves*

and had taken on a more industrial rather than agricultural air. The crucial period here is the reorganisation of the farm in the early second century. This shows all the hallmarks of Roman agriculture and suggests that the farm had been acquired by a veteran, or had been reorganised by a native farmer who was initiating new farming practices. The former seems the most likely explanation since the proximity of the farm to the fortress would suggest that it lay within the land owned by the city (its *territorium*). That such changes were widespread around Wroxeter is hinted at also in the regular pattern of plots identified on the north bank of the Bell Brook which excavation has shown were filled in in the early second century when the city's defences were extended across the Bell Brook valley (**32**). Again, the regular pattern of plots suggests small fields which, given their size, can only have been used to grow cash crops for market. Quite how far such reorganisation of the landscape extended around Wroxeter is not clear. Although there was no space within the fortress for market gardens, in the later city it will have been commonplace for nearly every house to have had some sort of garden or allotment on which to grow fresh food and the majority of these will have been inside the city walls or in their immediate vicinity.

The exploitation of the immediate hinterland in this way can be paralleled throughout the empire and was actively encouraged by the state through the allotment of land to retired soldiers either around an existing fortress or, on a grander scale, through the creation of a colony of citizens, as at Colchester or Gloucester. The purpose of this was two-fold: it would set the local population an example of how Roman life was led and if required would provide an emergency reserve of trained military personnel. As already shown, evidence for at least four soldiers who died at Wroxeter has been found in the form of tombstones and of these, three came from thoroughly Romanized areas such as northern Italy and southern Gaul (see **22**). They will have brought with them the Roman way of life, and an agricultural practice which may have stimulated the growing of different crops or will at least have improved agricultural regimes and techniques of animal husbandry. Some of this is detectable in other areas of Britain through the increasing size of animals for slaughter, for example, although the data from Wroxeter is still too patchy to test whether such improvements took place there also. Similarly, the introduction of new crops has not yet been proved through archaeobotany but there is growing evidence for the introduction of a considerable number of plant species during the Roman period of which sweet chestnut and the grape vine are perhaps the most well-known. Grape pips have been found at Wroxeter and, given the recent discovery of the first definite example of a British vineyard in Northampton, there may have been a vineyard in the vicinity of Wroxeter, though the pips might be from dried fruit imported from further south.

Moving further away from Wroxeter, radical reorganisation of the fields as seen at Duncote is less likely since these farms will have had little opportunity to exploit the static population offered first by the fortress and then later by the city. However, Wroxeter's impact on the landscape can be measured through the distribution and change in the settlement pattern. As in the Iron Age, it seems clear that the bulk of the rural population in the Roman period lived in enclosed farmsteads. A recent study of those in the Upper Severn has suggested that those which have rectilinear plans tend to cluster around Wroxeter and may thus belong to the Roman period, representing an intensification of agriculture and a growth in overall population for region. Certainly, fieldwalking of unexcavated examples has often found Roman pottery and other artefacts in association with them. This simple pattern is complicated by the fact that when excavated many of these enclosures seem to have been founded in the Iron Age and to have continued into the Roman period. Unfortunately, still too little is known of these sites to be certain that a simple equation between square plans and a Roman date can be relied on. There is also good evidence for believing that many of the curvilinear enclosures too are Roman in date and ultimately the variations in form may be a matter of personal whim and fashion rather than a choice between a Roman or native life style. The same may also be said of villas, which most people would define as farms built in Roman fashion with mosaics, a bath house and a rectilinear plan.

It might be expected that the retired soldiers farming in the vicinity of Wroxeter would construct Romanized buildings of this sort but remarkably few have been found in Shropshire and those that have been excavated have proved to be mostly late in date. Part of the difficulty is in actually seeing villas in the landscape in the first place: two have recently been discovered within metres of the city's defences but both were found by careful field survey after ploughing which identified dense clusters of pottery or building material. Still others are hinted at on modern farms near Wroxeter where fieldwalking has again found building material and pottery suggesting Roman buildings

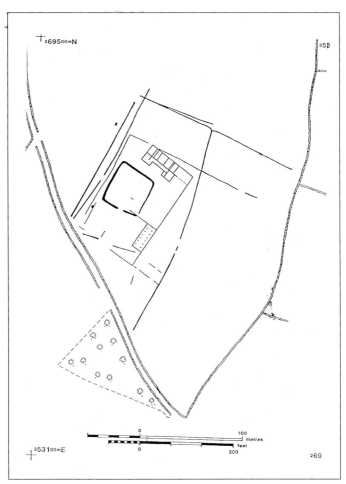

33 *A plot, from an aerial photograph, of the villa at Ashford Carbonell. The villa building is on one side of a courtyard, another side of which has an aisled ?barn. This complex in turn overlies a single-ditched rectangular enclosure, perhaps the Iron Age or early Roman predecessor of the villa*

lying in the vicinity of, or perhaps beneath, existing farms. Since the most common building material in Shropshire and Cheshire before the late seventeenth century was wood, it is likely that many of these villas will remain difficult to detect since they will not produce large quantities of rubble. Given these problems, it is probable that Wroxeter, like other Roman cities, did have an extensive network of Romanized farms in its vicinity, intermingled with a larger number of enclosed sites representing the longer-lived local traditions. Indeed, there are hints that the two site types may have co-existed or succeeded each other since at Ashford Carbonell a recently observed cropmark of an enclosure proved on closer examination to have a villa next to it (**33**) while at Berwick Alkmund Park an enclosed site has produced a second-century bath house whose associated villa has yet to be discovered. Are we seeing at these sites the replacement of a local farmer by a Roman settler or, more likely, given the remoteness of the sites, the local farmers changing their life-style from the old fashioned native roundhouse to the new, and far more comfortable, Roman villa?

4 The foundation and growth of the City

Of the 180 acres (78ha) enclosed by Wroxeter's defences, only three are occupied by its grandiose public buildings. Eighty per cent of the area of these buildings has been excavated compared with about 1 per cent of the remaining area. Consequently, we have a very detailed picture of the evolution of the city's public buildings yet know much less about how or where its population lived. This problem becomes even more acute when considering the early history of the city which lies more deeply buried beneath the later remains. Much of our knowledge of the city and its buildings has come from the superb sets of aerial photographs taken since the Second World War (see **20**). Fortunately, the largely sandy sub-soil under much of the city means that stone-founded buildings tend to show up remarkably clearly, appearing to provide a complete city plan. Despite this there were always blank areas at the periphery apparently devoid of buildings, even of roads, which have always given Wroxeter a half-empty appearance. This in turn has led to the conclusion that the city was ultimately a failure. It has been suspected for some time that these empty spaces were more illusory than real and in 1995 the opportunity arose through the Wroxeter Hinterland Project, a research project designed to look at Wroxeter and its impact on the surrounding countryside, to test whether the blank areas were indeed devoid of structures.

The early medieval shrinkage of Wroxeter has meant that the interior of the city has remained undisturbed except by agriculture. Thus the modern-day appearance of the site is of undulating pasture, an environment ideal for modern geophysics, the method of detecting buried structures using various scientific instruments (**34**). Principal among these are the fluxgate gradiometer, a device for measuring the minute variations in the earth's magnetic field caused by buried remains such as walls, pits, ditches and other man-made disturbances, and the resistivity meter which passes a small electrical current through the ground and measures the varying resistance to that current caused by buried archaeology. The plots of both methods look like x-ray photographs, although a considerable degree of skill and experience is required to interpret the results. The technologies used in the survey were not novel: earlier versions of both machines had been tested at Wroxeter over the past 40 years, most significantly during the 1950s when a magnetometer survey located the remains of a tile kiln on the Severn flood-plain at the foot of the river cliff below the city ramparts. The difference is that modern machines can now log and off-load their data onto computers so that the results are available instantly

34 *Dr Albert Hesse of the French national scientific research centre (CNRS) using an automated resistivity meter of his own design in the field south of the baths, August 1995*

and the resulting plots can be further enhanced and clarified using computer software. Thus, for the first time, a comprehensive survey of the city could be contemplated.

The results of the survey exceeded even the most optimistic forecasts, as can be judged from the illustrations shown here. Not only do they redefine the known buildings within the central core of the city but they have also added whole city blocks on the periphery, leaving few blank areas (**colour plates 3 & 5**). In addition, the survey has been able to pinpoint areas where industrial activity may have taken place, involving kilns or industrial hearths which give particularly clear magnetic signals. The identification of such features allows some assessment of the location of industrial zones within the city. The most illuminating technique has been a complete gradiometry survey, the first time that an entire Roman city has been mapped in this way. At its best, it shows the houses, shops and temples of the city as clearly as in the aerial photographs; elsewhere the results are less clear due to the intensity of occupation so that, although one can see that a considerable amount of human activity has taken place, the overlapping of these activities means that the plots are confused. The geophysical plots have once and for all settled the question of whether Wroxeter was sparsely occupied or not: the city proves to be densely occupied right up to its defences. Of course, as we shall see, this does not mean to say that it was always densely settled. There must have been fluctuations in the population which meant that some areas were occupied and then later abandoned. Furthermore, the geophysical map, like that derived from aerial photographs, only tells us where buildings and activity were located within the city. It can neither date that activity nor its duration: only excavation will reveal the pattern and

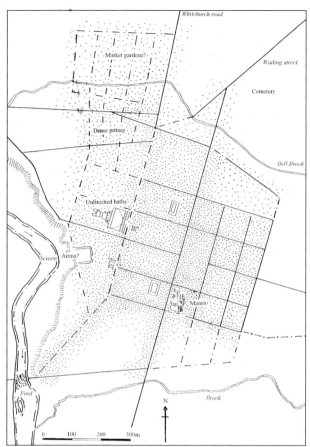

35 *A plan of the known extent of the early city, c.90–150*

sequence of occupation. Excavation would also without doubt add a large number of buildings with more ephemeral evidence in the upper levels which the geophysical surveys do not pick up easily, while for deeply-buried structures only ground-penetrating radar can supply any geophysical information.

The transition from military rule to civilian life at Wroxeter seems to have been smoothly accomplished. The army cleared out the fortress and demolished most of its buildings, although as we shall see there is evidence that some continued in use. Despite the warning of the Boudican revolt, the defences of the fortress and those on the southern lip of the Bell Brook were thrown down, but its street grid was retained to form the nucleus of the new city – its regularity was one of the factors that enabled the identification of the position of the fortress in the mid-1970s. In this, Wroxeter follows the example of other civilian cities founded on the sites of fortresses, such as Colchester. There were modifications to the street grid, however, including the creation or extension of new roads beyond the positions of the fortress walls so that the areas to the north, west and south could be formally integrated with the new city (**35**). The main road through the city was still on the line of the *via principalis* but later in the city's life, perhaps when the new main thoroughfare was created one *insula* to the west, this road line was partly built over, a new street being laid out to the west.

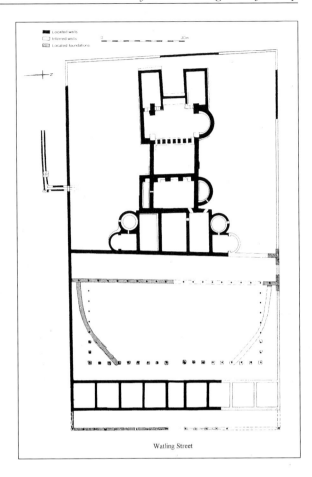

36 *A restored plan of the unfinished*
baths beneath the forum

Watling Street

It is likely that the nucleus of the early city thus lay at the heart of the former fortress, on either side of this main road. There must have been some sort of forum, which combined the functions of the tribal administration and judiciary with that of a market place. The precise location of this is unknown as the area has never been excavated but the headquarters of the fortress itself would have been a suitable substitute and it may be that that building was the city's first forum. Dr Graham Webster has also suggested that a row of columns, visible on air photographs of this area, may be evidence for early baths here, but this colonnade could equally belong to the forum itself and it is perhaps more likely that the early city baths were those started on the site of the later city forum, two *insulae* to the west.

The baths found beneath the later forum pose a number of difficult questions which are not easily answered. The evidence, however, is relatively straightforward. When Donald Atkinson excavated the site in the 1920s he was amazed to find beneath the forum a massive bath house which, it became apparent, had never been completed (**36**). This building dated to the late first century and must belong therefore either to the later stages of the fortress or to the early city. Its plan was quite unlike that of the public baths subsequently built on the other side of the Watling Street. The bath building was fronted by an open exercise yard, originally intended to be semi-circular but then completed as a

73

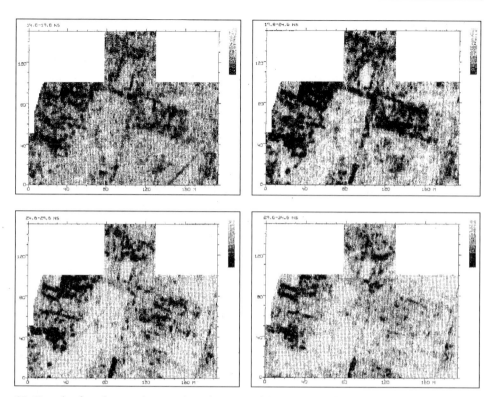

37 *Four plots from the ground-penetrating radar survey of August 1995. These show the site at between about 0.15m–0.6m depth (14.8–34.6 nano-seconds). The plots are orientated so that north is to the left. The intersection of the streets is clear in all the plots. The pale rectangular area adjacent to the crossroads is the church-like building, complete with an apsidal east end. At the left of each plot is a large courtyard house which has a projecting apsidal room at the south-west corner (compare with 43). Right of the crossroads is a large rectangular building with an internal courtyard. This persists throughout all the plots and must therefore be an early building, perhaps dating to the time of the fortress. In all but the last images, two parallel modern water pipes cut diagonally across the site – their presence varies since they are at differing depths*

rectangle with an internal colonnade and, flanking the east side, undressing rooms, an apsidal warm room and a circular sweat room. Alternatively, one could go straight into an unheated room with a plunge pool at either end and, beyond, a warm and then a hot room, the latter with two projecting furnaces. The whole edifice was set within an enclosed service yard. The plan of the baths, which has parallels throughout the north-western provinces, has its closest antecedents in military bath houses found in fortresses, perhaps indicating that these baths were intended for use with Wroxeter's fortress rather than its early city. This would certainly explain why they were never finished since, if the army had moved on to Chester before the baths were completed, it is likely that the nascent city would have had neither the financial resources nor access to competent engineers to carry the project through. There may also have been an element of fashion involved. The early unfinished baths were already quite old-fashioned in concept, not least in the provision for a large open exercise yard, a feature which locals would have realised would have been of limited use for much of the year. If the baths were part-constructed by the army therefore, but never completed, the city would have been left with a useless set of walls and foundations, and no public baths, until the construction of the new baths in the mid-second century (chapter 5). An alternative scenario is that the city could have started the project in a burst of enthusiasm but then found that they had neither the resources nor the technical skill to complete it. This, however, does not square with construction of the later baths and forum which seems to have been carried through with little technical difficulty only 30 years later.

A number of other buildings from the early city may be identified on the evidence of aerial photography and geophysical survey. For example, two large rectangular courtyard buildings, one lying between the *via principalis* and the later Watling Street, and the other situated to the north of the modern road running diagonally across the city. Both are slightly larger than other city houses and have rooms of equal size around all four sides. Geophysical survey has provided an insight into the history of the first of these buildings with automated resistivity survey showing that there was a broad porch supported on posts or columns at the south end and ground-penetrating radar showing that this was a particularly long-lived building (**37**). Careful plotting of these buildings using a computer has shown that both lie slightly askew to the city street grid but align perfectly with the defences of the legionary fortress. Both also lie in similar positions within the fortress suggesting that these buildings may have been long-lived survivors of the fortress adapted to civilian use, perhaps as inns or hotels, given the fact that the rooms appear to be identical in size. Similar arguments can be used to explain why a single granary, of obvious military type, is visible on aerial photographs to the east of the *via principalis* in the northern half of the fortress (see **20**). Such a building would still have been useful in a city, especially if the large enclosure within which it lies was indeed the livestock market (*forum boarium*), as is argued in chapter 5.

One last building may be identified from this early phase of the city's life. It lies to the east of the first large rectangular building discussed above, on the east side of the *via principalis*. Its plan is known both from aerial photographs (which give a partial plot) and the recent geophysical survey (**38**). These show two conjoined courtyards, the one to the north about 45m square (including the surrounding rooms) and the other about 45m x 35m. Rooms of regular size are placed around all sides of the second courtyard but the first has rooms of more irregular size and shape. To the east of the first courtyard building, that is away from the main street, is a long rectangular building with a projecting room at the south end, almost certainly a bath house. It is attached to the courtyard building and must be part of the same complex. What marks this set of buildings out is its complexity and the fact that, alone of all the buildings within the area of the former fortress, it is not aligned on the existing street grid but at an angle to it. Although only excavation will fully elucidate this building, on analogy with similar buildings in other cities this is probably Wroxeter's *mansio*. This was a building provided for the benefit of the imperial postal system, with one in every city or town and at intervals of about 20 miles along the major routes between towns. Here, imperial couriers, usually soldiers on secondment from the legions, could change their horses, and find a bed and a bath for the night. In rural areas, the *mansio* often provided the spur for the development of a new settlement since traders were guaranteed a market. In Cornovian territory, the *mansio* at Wall provides a good example of such a development, and there may well have been similar buildings at Whitchurch and Wilderspool.

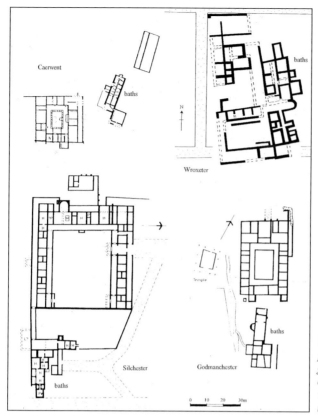

38 *A composite plan of Wroxeter's putative* mansio *based on geophysical and aerial photographic evidence, with comparative* mansio *plans from other British towns and cities*

Excavation has provided some insight into the houses that the first inhabitants of the city lived in. Bushe-Fox, excavating along the line of the new road which later became the Watling Street, identified a number of timber houses aligned gable-end onto the street and apparently without solid façades (see **26**). If so, these may well have been simple shops with accommodation in the rear as have been found in London and other British cities and all over the Roman empire. Atkinson too found fragmentary evidence for simple timber buildings beneath the forum, as did Kenyon beneath the town house she excavated south of the baths, but the most important evidence for this early phase has come from the excavations below the *macellum*. Here Graham Webster found a large rectangular or E-shaped building aligned along Watling Street. The rear wall of this apparently reused the wall of a military stone-footed building but the other walls were of closely-set posts with wooden panels between them. Internal divisions suggest that this large building may have been divided into a number of individual premises with a common foof, an arrangement which has been argued for similar early buildings at *Verulamium*. None of the substantial stone-built or stone-footed houses excavated so far within the city, however, appear to belong to this early phase and it may well be that the substantial part of the city's population were traders, craftsmen, and the relatively poor who had been attracted to the new settlement in the hope of improvement. Nonetheless, there must have been families of substance too, especially the retired legionaries and their descendants, who presumably formed a substantial proportion of

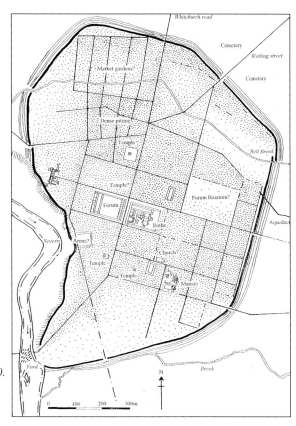

39 *A plan of the mature city, c.150-500. The extent and density of settlement shown is based on the gradiometry plot (see* **colour plate 3***)*

the city council (*ordo*), and the tribal aristocracy who will have settled in the city in the hope of social and financial advancement. If so, their houses lie elsewhere, perhaps in the centre of the town to the east of the areas excavated to date.

The full extent of the built-up area of the early city cannot yet be determined. Clearly, the area of the fortress was probably the most densely settled area, and the excavations of Bushe-Fox, Atkinson and Kenyon have demonstrated that the early settlement extended along both sides of the later Watling Street towards the modern village where an early glass-working site is known. It is probable too that further houses occupied the tract of land between the north side of the fortress and the southern lip of the Bell Brook valley, where the *canabae* once stood. To the north of the Bell Brook, as outlined in the previous chapter, a series of regular plots hint at market gardens associated with the early city and there may have been buildings associated with these too.

When the city defences were constructed in the mid-second century, all of the area outlined above was included, encompassing the whole of the valley of the Bell Brook north of the fortress as well as a large area between the southern edge of the fortress and a small unnamed stream a few hundred metres away. The city thus created was roughly oval, encompassing 180 acres (78ha), making it the fourth largest city in Roman Britain (**39**). The construction of the defences and the new civic buildings demanded a reorganisation of the city's road system which under the earlier fortress and city had seen the principal road turning south before it crossed Bell Brook. The new main

77

40 *The inscription from the entrance to the forum*

thoroughfare of the city was located one grid further west so that it ran along the line of the western defences of the former fortress. This meant that the line of Watling Street had to be extended to cross the Bell Brook where it joined the road coming south from Whitchurch. As will be shown in chapter 5, this main thoroughfare was made all the more impressive within the central part of the city by colonnades, behind which were the city's main public buildings including the forum, public baths, and perhaps the main temple. Equally impressive in their own way were the city's defences which consisted of a substantial bank and ditch system crowned with a wooden palisade and parapet. There is some evidence too that there may have been stone gates, at least at the main Watling Street entrance. The new public buildings and the defences were symbols of the city's success and emphasised to the visitor the confidence of the tribe in their new capital.

The sheer size and scale of the newly-established city has often been seen as slightly incongruous compared with the perceived poverty of the Cornovian countryside and it has until recently been accepted wisdom that Wroxeter was a failure, its vast walls encompassing only a handful of buildings. In the light of the geophysical survey, this vision is no longer tenable, and from earlier chapters it will be remembered that the poverty of Cornovian territory is an illusion suggested by the absence of a distinctive tribal material culture. Nonetheless, it has been argued in the past that the enclosure of the Bell Brook valley, which represents an enlargement of the city area by nearly 89 acres (36ha, or about 46 per cent of the enclosed area), arose from the direct intervention of the imperial government, and specifically that of the Emperor Hadrian himself. Dr Graham Webster in particular has suggested that the forum inscription itself is proof that the Emperor had visited the city during his brief visit to Britain in 121-2, since it is of such quality that only a mason travelling in his entourage would have been able to carve to such a high standard (**40**). This conclusion has recently been questioned by conservators working on the restoration of the inscription who have pointed out a number of errors in cutting and laying out which indicate that the work is provincial rather than imperial. Graham Webster also believes that Hadrian's interest in Wroxeter lay in the Emperor's perception that Wroxeter was the westernmost of the *civitas* capitals of his Empire. The truth or otherwise of this theory is difficult to judge in the absence of direct evidence but the parallels for such dramatic imperial intervention are few. Indeed, from the letters of the younger Pliny to Hadrian's predecessor, Trajan, we can see that imperial help for provincial cities was not readily forthcoming, presumably as this would open the floodgates for other cities to

41 *The east end of the Bell Brook valley from the point where the Watling Street crosses the brook*

promote their interests. Far more likely, if Hadrian had ever visited Wroxeter, would have been a public gesture such as the remittance of local taxes for a period so that the community, instead of rendering locally-collected taxes and tolls to the provincial procurator, could instead use them to finance new public buildings.

If the *deus ex machina* of imperial whim is rejected as the reason for Wroxeter's sudden burst of building activity, we are still left to decide why such a thorough-going restructuring of the city was considered necessary. The inclusion of the Bell Brook valley within the enclosed area is particularly difficult to understand since it made the newly-established defensive line of the city unnecessarily difficult to protect. This was because, although at the western end the Bell Brook has a relatively flat profile, on the east side the stream lies in a steep defile which cannot have been easily crossed by the defences (**41**). A parallel to this sort of development is the extension of London's defences to take in the whole of the Walbrook valley, but the two cities can hardly be compared since London, as the provincial capital, has a very distinctive pattern of expansion. As we have seen, Wroxeter's earlier defensive line had been established on the southern crest of the Bell Brook but for some reason it became imperative to enclose the whole valley. Geophysical and aerial survey shows that this area was never extensively developed for housing, the only buildings being those on the main street frontages and those just inside the north-eastern defences. The rest of the enclosed area consists of the regular plots, thought to be market gardens seen mostly north of the Bell Brook at the north-western corner of the city, and to the south of these plots, a very dense scatter of pits which are presumably related to some sort of industrial activity, such as tanning, in which pits are an integral part of the process.

Two suggestions may be made to account for the enclosure of the valley within the city walls. First the city council, carried away in a burst of unjustified optimism,

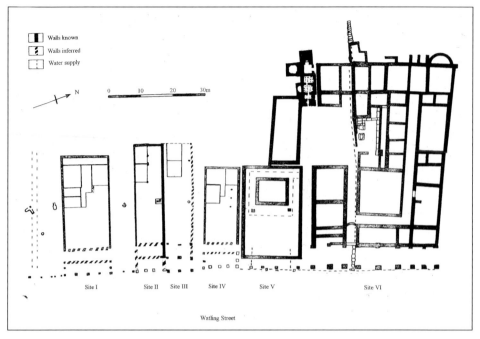

Walls known
Walls inferred
Water supply

N

0   10   20   30m

Site I   Site II   Site III   Site IV   Site V   Site VI

Watling Street

42 *Strip-buildings and town houses excavated by Bushe-Fox. Between Sites IV and VI is a classical-style temple (Site V)*

enclosed a very large area for expansion hoping that the blank areas would be filled by sustained growth in the city's population. Second, the city council may have decided to include all the suburban development within the walls, including the industrial areas and market gardens. This was not the usual practice in Roman cities and towns but in this case the city council may have been following the much more ancient (and to them familiar) pattern of hillfort development. The hillforts of the *Cornovii* are noted both for their large size and for additional enclosures which, it has been argued, were for livestock or for industrial activity. At Old Oswestry, for example, a series of rectangular compounds which may have been for penning livestock was added to the defences on one side (see **14**). For the city council of Wroxeter, presumably largely composed of native aristocrats, it will have seemed second nature to have included both housing and suburban development within Wroxeter's walls to both define and protect the city and its industry. This being so, the actual line of the defences was dictated by the natural topography of the site so that it included both sides of the Bell Brook valley and, to the south, the small unnamed stream south of the ford.

The houses of the mature city are much better known than those of the earliest period, but even so excavation of houses in the past has been patchy and often rather summary. Nonetheless, enough has been learnt to show that Wroxeter's houses conform well to the known development of those in other Romano-British cities and this allows us to compare them together. The most comprehensive excavation of city houses at Wroxeter was undertaken just to the north of the village and south-west of the ruins of the public baths by Bushe-Fox in the years 1912–4. He found a series of long houses, aligned with their narrow ends on the main street and running back within regular-sized plots and with open yards beyond (**42**). Such buildings are commonly referred to as strip-buildings and have many parallels both within Britain and on the continent. Most are interpreted as the houses of craftsmen or artisans, the first part of the house forming the shop with accommodation behind and above for the family and the storage of raw materials or finished products.

Strip-buildings were relatively unsophisticated in design and were constructed with walls of clay supported by a wooden-panelled framework. The excavator found some examples of daub with a patterned finish to receive plaster so despite the simple technology these houses are likely to have been quite comfortable, a picture confirmed by the plain concrete floors in some of them. Access to the rooms behind the frontage was gained either through the front room or via a passage alongside the house. Behind each house was a long open plot used as a yard or as a garden. Occupants often dug their own wells in these plots to provide ready access to water although some houses were connected to the mains water supply which ran in a stone channel along the street frontage. Sluices were provided for these houses and householders would be allowed to divert water into their properties at certain times during the day. Although each house developed individually, there is a suggestion of a unified approach to the appearance of the façades of the buildings since the excavator found evidence for a colonnade which would have both sheltered those shopping and provided an impressive appearance to the run of houses in keeping with their situation on the principal thoroughfare of the city.

One of the houses was found to have undergone a sequence of development which clearly showed that its occupants had acquired a neighbouring property and had then linked the two to provide a grander, courtyard-style house. Later additions to this complex saw a small baths suite added at the south-west corner, well away from the street frontage, despite the presence of the public baths almost directly across the street from the house. Of particular interest in this set of buildings was evidence for private religion in the form of a household shrine (*lararium*) and the small pipe-clay figurines which would have adorned it. The intermingling of private and public religion is also emphasised by the classical-style stone temple built next to this building on the site of a house burnt down in the disastrous fire which destroyed the forum in the late second century. Altogether this group of buildings provides strong evidence for a street scene very similar to that which might be found in any other city in the empire.

The buildings described thus far lay in the middle range of what might be expected from a city like Wroxeter: there would have been many humbler dwellings such as simple cottages and one- or two-room structures which lay behind the street frontages or at the periphery of the city and which housed the urban poor but none of these has yet been detected at Wroxeter and their presence and appearance can only be guessed at. More visible from the air or from geophysics, even if not yet excavated, are the isolated corridor houses which are to all appearances identical to the simpler country villas known throughout the north-western provinces. They are characterised by a row of more or less equally-sized rooms, some with underfloor heating, the end rooms of which project to allow a corridor or verandah to be created at the front. It may be expected that such houses, set back as they are from the street frontage, would stand within gardens. A single example of this type of house has been excavated in the south-east quarter of the city where at least one room with a hypocaust was found, amongst

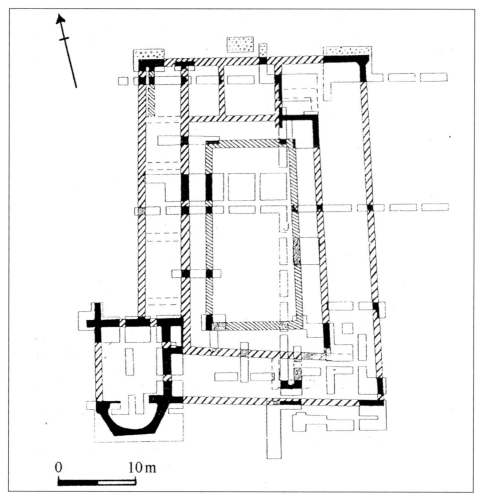

0   10 m

43 *A restored plan of the courtyard house south of the baths excavated by Dame Kathleen Kenyon in 1952–3. This plan shows the 'grey building period' when a projecting dining room was added at the south-west corner. Only the walls coloured black were actually excavated*

the floor supports of which were fragments of a mosaic and elaborate plaster decoration hinting that these modest buildings were well built and comfortable. Another, as yet unexcavated, example just to the east of the baths is known from geophysics. This has an L-shaped plan with at least four rooms, the northernmost room having a curved (apsidal) wall indicating its use as a dining room.

More impressive still are the courtyard houses which can be observed in several forms on the aerial photographs, one of which was sampled in excavation by Dame Kathleen Kenyon and Dr Graham Webster in 1952–3. This particular example, lying immediately south of the baths, was identified in an aerial photograph taken by Dr J. K. S. St Joseph in the late 1940s, one of the first of Wroxeter's buildings to be spotted from the air and thus a good candidate for testing the correlation between what was seen on the photograph and what was found in excavation (**43**). Limited time and resources meant that the examination consisted only of a number of excavated box-trenches located over the walls and within the rooms. The evidence showed that the house had been built in the second century in red 'Keele Beds' sandstone as a simple four-sided building with an internal courtyard facing onto the adjacent street. The house was rebuilt in the fourth century with the addition of a projecting room with a curved, apsidal, wall, the new masonry being signalled by a change to grey sandstone 'Hoar Edge Grit'. Once again there was evidence for painted plaster within the rooms, the patterns of which were not capable of reconstruction but which showed that the house had been well finished inside.

A similar house has been observed both in geophysical survey and as a cropmark about 50m to the east of the building just described where it occupies a raised position in the field. The evidence of the radar survey over this building suggests that it too acquired a projecting room in the south-west corner at a later stage in its life. Such rooms can be interpreted as dining rooms (*triclinia*) and their extension beyond the line of the house implies that the occupants had a garden around the building which could be admired from such rooms. A number of other courtyard buildings similar to those already discussed are known from other areas of the city.

The largest of Wroxeter's houses are to be found on the western side of the city close to the river cliff, taking advantage of the prevailing south-westerly wind to blow noxious smells and smoke away from them. Two houses in particular stand out, neither of which has been excavated. The first is a huge courtyard house occupying a major junction just to the north-west of the forum. Its sheer size marks it out from other courtyard houses but its plan is simply a larger example of those already discussed. The other lies further west, virtually at the edge of the city but commanding fine views of the Severn plain west of Wroxeter (see **21**). Here, a large corridor house straddles one of the roads leading from the forum. At least two dozen rooms can be seen with extensions at either end to create a verandah. It is not difficult to imagine this building, with its imposing setting and its deliberate positioning over one of the city's streets, as the residence of one of the leading citizens of the city or tribe.

Although few of the private houses have been excavated, enough has been found to demonstrate that they were decorated with well-executed wall paintings, though none have so far proved to include figures. The normal patterns are solid panels of bright colours, some imitating marble effects. The larger houses were often equipped with hypocausts in at least one of the rooms and the very grandiose examples, such as those excavated by Bushe-Fox and Thomas Telford, had private bath suites. Mosaics are comparatively rare in Wroxeter with most of the known examples being fourth century in date, but this perception may be misleading due to the lack of excavation within the city. Most houses were built in either wood, cob, or stone although it is conceivable that even the stone foundations at Wroxeter represent no more than the footings for timber-framed or cob superstructures. Certainly, Shropshire and Cheshire abound in stone-footed, timber-framed medieval houses and only very wealthy Viroconians would have been able to build a house completely in stone. Indeed, the very clarity of the house plans at Wroxeter argues strongly that the buildings were half-timbered since the rubble from collapsed stone houses would have obscured the plans of the buildings from the geophysical surveys.

5 Wroxeter's public buildings

Due to their extensive, almost continuous, excavation since 1859 Wroxeter's public buildings are far more comprehensively understood than its private dwellings. This long campaign has had its drawbacks, however, in the destruction, by weathering, of much of the detail of the public baths which have been exposed for display (see chapter 1). Nonetheless, the history of the buildings discovered by these excavations demonstrates extremely well both the confidence and wealth of Wroxeter's community. Wroxeter's civic centre lay on either side of Watling Street with the forum on the west side and the baths on the east (**colour plate 6**). It is suggested here that the major public temple lay to the north of the forum and that all these buildings, and certainly the street façades to the south, were unified by a colonnade. In addition to these public buildings, the city council also provided and maintained the city's markets, temples, cemeteries, defences, water supply, and road system. The money for these projects ultimately came from the taxes collected from the tribe so that the city was in a very real sense the expression of tribal identity in concrete, stone, and wood.

Excavation has shown that the forum was the first major public building constructed. This building has a complex history in that, as seen in the previous chapter, there was an uncompleted baths building on the site which, for reasons that we cannot know, was never completed. Although this decision was made, it left the city council with the problem of what to do with a half-finished building. Their bold decision was to start again with a new baths which, owing to the completely new style of plan, had to be on a fresh site. Cleverly, the engineer designing the forum decided to use the eastern half of the unfinished baths, comprising the row of shops, its external portico and internal colonnade with a grand entrance, to form the front half of the forum. The western half, built over the unfinished baths, used some of that building's wall lines, which meant that the work could be carried out very quickly: excavated pottery and coins show that work on the forum began in about 120 and the beautifully-cut forum inscription commemorates the dedication of the building between winter 129 and autumn 130 with a spring or summer completion likely (see **40**).

The rapid progress made with the forum is in stark contrast to the baths which, as we shall see, took over thirty years to build. Quite why this discrepancy exists is not clear but several suggestions can be made to explain why the forum was completed so quickly. First, the hiatus of about thirty years between stopping the construction of the

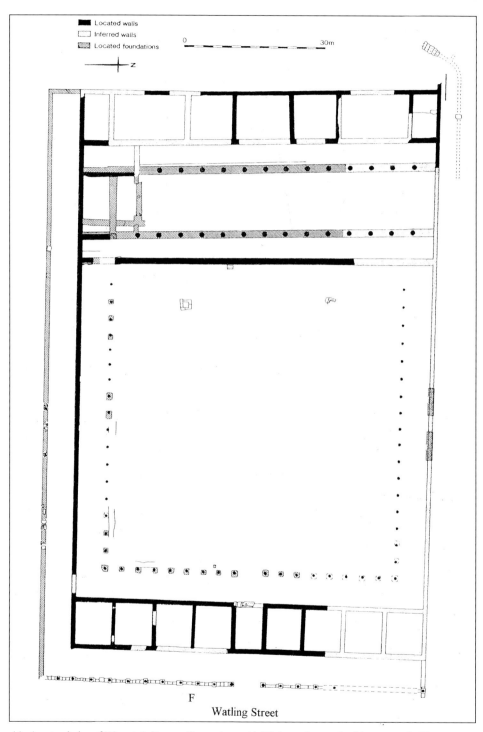

44 *A restored plan of Wroxeter's Forum. Comparison with **36** shows that much of the courtyard of the unfinished baths was reused to create the Forum piazza and shops. The position of the gutter find is marked at F*

unfinished baths house and the decision to reuse the site as the new forum meant that sufficient revenue had accumulated to allow building to progress quickly. Furthermore, the clever reuse of elements of the unfinished building will again have cut time and costs. Alternatively, if the Emperor Hadrian had visited Wroxeter, he might have remitted taxes for a fixed period, as discussed in chapter 4, in which case there would have been an accumulation of capital rapid enough to allow the swift construction. Whatever the precise circumstances of funding, the pragmatic solution to the knotty problem of providing the city with a modern, up-to-date baths and forum was a wonderful example of how an imaginative approach to the problem could derive a splendid public building from what potentially could have been a disastrous mistake, and is a tribute to the inventiveness of the (unknown) architect.

The forum was one of the most important civic buildings in the city, embodying as it did the tribe's identity. It was a massive building which filled an entire city block (*insula*) and had a plan similar to many other fora in Britain, with a large internal courtyard 74m by 64m in size surrounded by an internal colonnade and fronted by a row of shops, four on each side of the grand entrance with, on the west side of the courtyard, a basilica, behind which was a set of rooms (**44**). Its role within the city was both as its commercial centre, the courtyard being the city's main market square, and as the administrative and judicial centre both for the city and the tribe as a whole.

The basilica, as large and impressive as that built on the baths *insula*, was where the two annually-appointed local magistrates held court, and where the governor would have held judicial trials on the occasions when he visited the city. These trials took place within the tribunal, a raised dais at the south end of the basilica isolated from the rest of the building both by its height and by the balustrade around it. Here the magistrates would sit under the gaze of the image of the Emperor which was placed here to witness proceedings. The rest of the hall was less formally used: one can imagine lawyers and their clients strolling within the nave awaiting their cases, or meetings and transactions taking place, since contracts could only be legally binding if they were witnessed in the presence of the image of the Emperor. The basilica was probably entered from a flight of steps in the centre of the long east side but doorways also existed at the ends of the courtyard colonnade. Thus, unlike the baths basilica, on entering one saw the interior of the building from the side rather than from the end. Directly opposite the main door was a series of doors leading to seven unequally-sized rooms beyond the west aisle. These had a number of functions but probably all related to the administration of the city and tribe. The large central room, directly opposite the entrance, was almost certainly the shrine (*sacellum*) which will have contained a statue of the Emperor and perhaps another personifying the tribe itself or the tribe's favoured god or goddess. The other rooms will have fulfilled a number of other roles: those at the southern end of the range will probably have included the city council debating chamber (*curia*) and treasury (*aerarium*) whilst one or perhaps two others were used by the annual magistrates. The northernmost room in the range was almost certainly the record office (*tabularium*) since, when the forum burnt down between 165–75, inkwells and part of an auxiliary soldier's discharge certificate recording his grant of citizenship were found in the ashes. The latter item, of crucial importance to its owner for establishing his Roman citizenship, would have been lodged in the record office for safe-keeping. This room could only be entered through the room adjacent to it and was perhaps the office of the

45 *A reconstruction drawing by Amédée Forestier in 1925 of the Watling Street and Forum in use. Although some of the detail can be faulted, it vividly conveys the bustle of the city in its heyday*

city clerk. The decoration of this building would have been at least as elaborate as that of the baths but little survived or was detected when it was excavated other than fragments of painted plaster which can be reconstructed as panels of bright primary colours, since the building had apparently been extensively robbed after its disuse. The courtyard would originally have been paved or gravelled and two masonry bases near the basilica attested to the presence of life-sized bronze statues, probably of emperors, fragments of which were found nearby. One statue base survives, crudely inscribed *Bono Reipublicae Natus*, 'Born for the good of the State', a formula usually used on statues of Emperors. On market days, stalls would have been set out both in the courtyard and in the external porticoes on the north, south and east sides. The presence of stalls is dramatically proved by the famous portico gutter find described in chapter 3.

Within a few decades of the completion of the forum, however, a disastrous fire swept through the building, destroying the west range, along with the stalls in the portico, and extending southwards to engulf the row of city houses adjacent to the complex. A date of about 165–75 is provided by the names of the potters on both the unused samian vessels and the rims of the mixing bowls found in the forum gutter. A second fire, at the end of the third century, seems to have caused irreparable damage to the forum basilica which then appears to have been abandoned although it is likely that the row of shops on the west front and the forum courtyard continued in use.

The forum's importance to Wroxeter is manifest in the huge number of artefacts from all corners of the Empire which have been found in the city, in contrast to the much smaller percentage which filtered into the countryside. It is not difficult to imagine the square bustling with people of all kinds of ethnic and social background, especially on

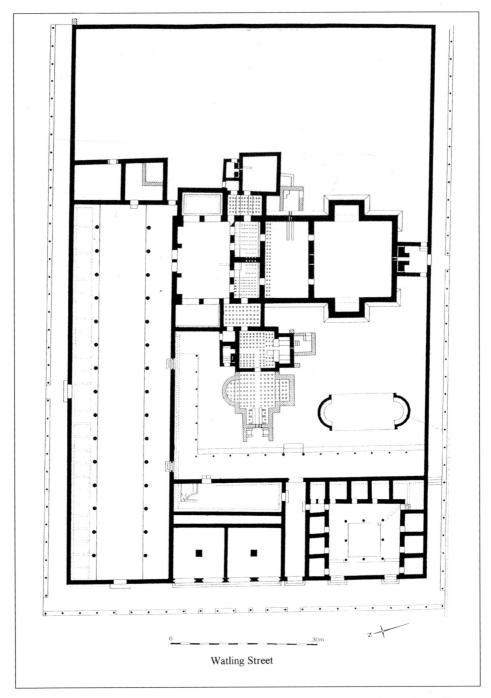

0   30m

Watling Street

46 *A restored plan of Wroxeter's public baths and* macellum *(bottom right corner), showing later additions (shaded), known drains (broken lines) and the positions of mosaic panels in the north aisle of the basilica (see* **colour plate 8***)*

market day when numerous stalls would have been set out with their wares for sale: brooches, beads, glassware, pottery, metal dishes, as well as all sorts of consumables: salads, vegetables, fruit, cheese, clothes and fabrics, and spices (**45**). Among the throng will have been the colourful characters associated with market days in any city: local farmers, merchants perhaps from the Rhineland, or the Greek-speaking east or from North Africa, peddlers, and quack doctors with their patent eye salves and other nostrums.

The other major public building provided for the new civic centre was the public baths. It too occupied a complete *insula*, this time to the east of Watling Street and directly opposite the forum (**46**). The earlier history of the baths site has not been fully investigated except beneath the bath's exercise yard and the nearby market hall (*macellum*) where Graham Webster was able to demonstrate a sequence beginning with a possible Iron Age enclosed farm which was replaced by the defences and barrack blocks of the legionary fortress. These were replaced by at least one building, perhaps sub-divided into several units, which belongs in the early city. This was demolished in the 120s to allow the digging of the massive foundation trenches necessary for the construction of the baths. Once the major foundations were in place, the floors of those rooms intended to have underfloor heating were excavated to the required depth. This could have been rapidly accomplished but on its completion work seems to have ceased for nearly thirty years. The reason for this hiatus is unclear and is especially odd given the rapid completion of the forum which apparently took no more than a decade to build despite being larger than the baths complex.

Two suggestions may be made to explain why the baths took so long to be built. First, the rapid construction of the city's forum and its defences may have exhausted the community's resources so that it was unable to continue the work, and second this lack of capital may have caused technical difficulties. Unlike the forum, the baths required the erection of concrete vaults for the main bath rooms. Construction in concrete must, however, be carried out swiftly: it cannot be laid piecemeal since that will not allow it to solidify as a single mass. It seems likely, therefore, that the community's resources being exhausted by the provision of the forum and the defences, a generation had to pass before sufficient capital had accumulated to allow work to continue. Despite the pause, the confidence of the city is evident in the laying of foundations for the complex, even though they may have known that work could not continue beyond that level for a considerable time. Alternatively, it could be argued that the hiatus was caused by some technical or even political problem.

When work did resume in the 150s, inspection pits were dug against some of the walls to check whether they had settled and one or two modifications were made to the design including moving the east end of the exercise hall (baths basilica) further to the east to insert a service door and redesigning the south-west corner of the *insula* to incorporate a market hall, another sign of the commercial confidence of the *Cornovii*. It was these modifications, perfectly understandable in the circumstances of such a complicated building, that have in the past been misinterpreted as being evidence for an early forum beneath the baths.

Once construction began again in earnest, the buildings were rapidly completed. The plan chosen for the baths was a simple one using the rectangular plot to best advantage by aligning the exercise hall parallel with the northern street and placing the shorter baths block at the south-east corner of the exercise hall so that it took up the centre of the *insula*. An external colonnade was provided on three sides to enhance the grandeur of the buildings and allow people to shelter from the weather and to shop at stalls set up there. On the west side, that facing onto the main thoroughfare, the Watling Street, lay first the main entrance to the basilica, then two possible shops or taverns with, behind them, the city latrine and then next to them the *macellum*, the shops and *macellum* being separated by a broad passage leading to the open exercise yard (*palaestra*) of the baths. This was itself colonnaded and had an open-air bathing pool (*natatio*) in one corner (**colour plate 7**). The eastern part of the *insula*, which was apparently only accessible from the north-south street which bounded it and was cut off from public access by the bulk of the baths buildings, must have been the service yard where the considerable supplies of fuel and material required to run the baths was stored. No exact parallel for these baths have been found but buildings with similar plans existed at nearby Chester and at Xanten (*Colonia Ulpia Traiana*), Germany. Whilst the main entrances to the baths were provided on the Watling Street frontage, alternative doors were also provided in the north wall of the basilica and there were intercommunicating doors between the basilica and the exercise yard so that visitors had the choice of exercising indoors or outdoors according to the season.

The baths basilica, which was 250 Roman feet (74m) long, was of conventional design with colonnades (of 13 columns) separating the nave from the north and south aisles. The floor of the nave was of polished mortar with crushed tile (*opus signinum*) but the aisles were floored with dark blue and white geometric mosaic panels with a blue-green border along their entire length (**colour plate 8**). The panels were alternately broad and narrow, the narrow ones being located behind the columns and the broad between them. A strange feature of the building is that it was constructed on a gentle slope so that the east end was higher than the west. This was presumably a cost-cutting exercise since to level the site of the basilica would have involved considerable earth-moving but this also produced a subtle optical effect in that visitors entering the basilica at the main door would have seen along its whole length, the east end being at about eye level from the west door. In addition, it may also have helped the drainage of rainwater away from the building. The rest of the decorative scheme of the basilica is only partly known: the exterior walls were painted white with paired lines painted in red perhaps representing simple panels or false jointing whilst at window height the inside walls were painted an orange-red.

At the east end of the basilica two identically-sized rooms formed an annexe. These may have been either changing rooms or the workshops of those responsible for maintaining the fabric of the baths, as these rooms later demonstrably became. Nearby was the double door into the baths proper, the opening for which still survives today in the Old Work. This led into the unheated room of the baths, the *frigidarium*, and it is possible that people undressed in this room rather than in the annexe. The decoration of the room is known in some detail: it had a mosaic floor in blue and white whose precise design is unknown and of plain white mosaic in the flanking cold plunge pools. These pools also had wall mosaics decorated with a guilloche pattern but the other walls of the rooms were plastered and painted (although the designs are not known) and were embellished with stucco columns on the wall surviving as the Old Work. The ceiling, which consisted of a three-bay transverse barrel vault, was covered with plaster painted to represent a coffered ceiling (**colour plate 9**). In the south wall of the room were four doors. Those in the corners of the room led to identical flanking suites consisting of a rectangular warm room (*tepidarium*) and a square hot, dry room (*sudatorium*) with its attached furnace. The other two doors led into two separate rooms; bathers entered the left hand door to a small room, (*unctorium*), where they would apply scented oil to themselves or have it applied by their slaves or servants, and then progress into the main warm room (*tepidarium*) beyond and thence into the large hot, humid room (*caldarium*) where they could take a hot bath or cool themselves with cold water provided in the rectangular alcoves. When clean, they would retrace their steps to enter the right hand room where they could give themselves a final rinse before re-entering the unheated room.

Although very little of the decoration survived, it is known that the floor had mosaics and the walls and ceilings had painted plaster. There would have been large, double-glazed windows in the thick walls, the whole ensemble being suitably impressive. Outside in the exercise yard, a small bathing pool (*natatio*) was paved with fine-grained sandstone, typical of the care that was taken with the complex (**colour plate 7**). The remaining buildings of the *insula* were no less grand, even though we know relatively little about them. The market hall (*macellum*) was a two-storey courtyard building with shops on three sides, the fourth side fronting Watling Street and pierced by two entrances. Each side had three shops, all identical in size with the north-east corner room being divided into a narrow lobby with a staircase in the room beyond and, in the south-east corner, an L-shaped latrine. In the centre of the courtyard was an open space surrounded by dwarf columns carrying the upper floor. The upper floor may have had lock-ups associated with the premises beneath or could have been separate establishments. Finally, between the market hall and the baths basilica lay two identically-sized rooms both with a central pier supporting a vault. The open plan of these rooms, and parallels with other bathing establishments throughout the Empire, suggest these may have been taverns or bars. A narrow corridor lay between these rooms and the public latrine which lay on the west side of the baths exercise yard.

After about fifty years of use the western baths suite was extended, the hot, humid room being converted into a full baths suite by the addition of another furnace and a rectangular hot plunge on the south wall while, adjacent to the hot room, another square room was built with an apsidal north wall and a rectangular extension to the south. This new room was heated by a furnace built on its west side which abutted the portico. At the same time the outdoor pool, which given the climate cannot have been used all year round, was filled in. There is also evidence for modifications in the main baths suite, primarily in the addition of a subsidiary furnace on the east side to heat the warm room and in the encasing of the warm and hot rooms in a sandstone wall which may have extended to roof level. The purpose of this latter addition is not clear. It has been interpreted as an an attempt to support the walls which, given the sandy subsoil of the site, may have been inadequate to support the heavy vault. Another minor addition was also carried out on the eastern baths suite involving the addition of a small furnace to the south wall of the hot room but this was done some time after the jacketing wall had been built. The expansion of the baths suites suggest that bathing had become a popular recreation in the city and that the tribe had adopted this particular Roman activity with enthusiasm, a factor which played an important part in keeping the bath functioning into the fourth century (see chapter 6).

Wroxeter, in common with other market towns, must have had a livestock market, the *forum boarium*. This will have been in a different place from the forum since only one entrance to that complex is known, the grand public doorway with its bronze-sheathed wooden doors and inscription above, which could only be reached via the main east portico. In medieval and modern Shrewsbury as in other towns, livestock was driven through the streets to be sold, but to keep the mess and disorder to a minimum, such markets are usually located at the town's periphery. In Roman Wroxeter, the best candidate for the site of the cattle market is a large, rectangular enclosure 168m by 152m in size which lies north of the baths and whose site is currently occupied by the home ground of Wroxeter Rovers Football Club (see **11, 20**). The enclosure has long been known to archaeologists since its discovery in the early aerial surveys of the 1950s and its lack of buildings mean that the underlying ditch of the fortress and its associated granary can be glimpsed along with other more shadowy buildings. The site has been interpreted either as a religious enclosure (*temenos*), despite the fact that no temple has ever been seen in it, or as a secure compound to store taxes paid in kind (*annona*). Whilst the *annona* became important in the late Roman Empire, this does not explain how the area was used in the early life of the city. The identification of the compound as a livestock market rests on a number of factors: its huge size would fit in with our understanding of the paramount importance of livestock to the Cornovian economy, and topographically it is ideally located for such a use. It sits at the highest point in the city; perhaps too exposed for normal houses but certainly suitable for livestock. It also lies adjacent to the point where the aqueduct reached the city and thus there was a more than adequate supply of water at hand. Furthermore it was also close to a number of major routes into and out of the city. Finally, being downwind of much of the city, it would be unlikely to offend its neighbours.

In addition to catering for the material needs of its citizens and the wider tribe, the city council was also expected to provide for their spiritual needs. Religion in the early Empire was primarily the concern of the individual. The provision of household shrines at Wroxeter is attested archaeologically in the form of small niches to hold statues in either metal or pipe-clay, examples of which have also been found. There is also evidence for personal belief in the numerous designs seen on signet rings; the design of one at least has been interpreted as showing that its owner was a devotee of Isis. There were also places where one might worship publicly and where the great religious festivals would have been celebrated. As already mentioned, provision was made in the forum for the worship of the city's gods in the central room in the west range of the basilica and it is likely that here also sacrifices to the Emperor's *numen* or *genius* would be made, though this does seem rather modest provision for the religious life of the community and a more usual approach was for the city to provide a public temple where the whole population might congregate to observe the religious rituals of the year.

No such temple has been identified at Wroxeter but a suggestion for its location may be made. Ordinarily, the public temple was adjacent to the forum, as in London's first forum, or inside it, as at *Verulamium*, but both the baths and the forum at Wroxeter occupy the whole of their *insulae* leaving insufficient space for a temple in either area. The surrounding city blocks, examined both by aerial and geophysical surveys, have produced small-scale temples but nothing like a grand civic temple such as might be expected in a city of Wroxeter's size and importance. The only gap in our knowledge of

47 *The surviving fragments of the Jupiter column and an outline reconstruction of the complete monument. It may have stood in front of Wroxeter's main temple. The tallest fragment is 1.05m*

the city blocks lies in that *insula* immediately to the north of the forum, occupied since the mid-nineteenth century by farm buildings. Interestingly, when these buildings were being erected, the floor was lowered in one of them to provide a sunken-floored barn. In doing so, a row of square-cut column bases forming a colonnade was uncovered. Each had slots cut into their sides as though to take a balustrade of some kind. The colonnade was set back from the street frontage but was parallel to it. Square-cut column bases have been found nowhere else at Wroxeter and it may well be that their distinctive design, and the lavishness of the colonnade, indicates that they represent the colonnade in front of a temple. The bases were robbed out by the farmer and most now survive, upended and hollowed out as plant holders, although two did end up reused in the gateway of St Andrew's church in Wroxeter village, where they support large column shafts and elaborate capitals which may have been derived from the same site; one of the capitals certainly had unusual decoration which is recorded in an antiquarian illustration of 1853 but which has now been almost entirely lost through weathering (**colour plate 10**).

It is also possible that other fragments of sculpture, published at the same time as the capitals, were found originally at the farm buildings site. These were recognised as pieces of an elaborate free-standing monument known as a Jupiter Column and were first noted in the yard of William Oakley, whose house stood opposite the churchyard gate, but they may well have been derived from the farm buildings site (**47**). If the Jupiter Column fragments were indeed found there, it would strongly support the location of a temple. The Jupiter Column was a peculiarly Romano-Celtic religious monument. It was a free-standing column, usually on a square base with an octagonal drum above. Each of the twelve faces thus provided by the base and octagonal drum would be decorated with a different deity from the pantheon of gods. Above this rose the column shaft, its surface decorated in this instance first with raised crossed bands and then an overlapping scale-leaf pattern. The column was crowned with a large capital, often decorated with figures, as in the example from Cirencester. On the very top of the column, Jupiter was depicted either on a throne or on horseback riding down a fish-tailed earth-god, which may be interpreted as the triumph of good over evil. The whole would have been gaudily painted and presumably stood in front of the temple as a symbol of the deity's protection of the city and of his presence in the nearby temple. The form of the monument, and its confinement to the Celtic world, suggest that these stone columns replaced earlier wooden 'totem poles' which may once have adorned the pre-Roman temples of the Celts. Also to be found on the shaft were the figures of Bacchus, *putti* with baskets of grapes, and dancing *maenads*. Their presence attests to the popularity of bacchic images at Wroxeter in common with the rest of the empire, and is also confirmed by the small votive capital decorated with the bacchic motifs of bunches of grapes and a hare found near the Bell Brook in 1996 (**48**). Three other pieces of religious sculpture are known from the city, although their findspots are not all known. The first is an incomplete altar decorated with several figures in separate panels including a Pan-like figure, a seated woman in a dress (perhaps a mother-goddess), a goat or ibex, and a male figure holding a dish and *cornucopia* (probably the god *Bonus Eventus*). Another piece appears to be a pillar since it probably shows Mars on one face but has carved leaves on two of its other surfaces. Neither stone carries any inscription, however, so these identifications cannot be precise. A third stone shows a wheeled

48 *A small decorated capital found in the Bell Brook valley in 1996. It has large acanthus leaves on the corners and, on the complete side, a hare. On the only other surviving side, a bunch of grapes is represented. Both symbols may be associated with the god Bacchus (Dionysius)*

phallus pulling a chariot filled with phalli. This last piece presumably is a good-luck symbol rather than a religious carving.

Of the city's other temples, only one has been excavated. This lay south of the forum and was a conventional classical style temple with a four column façade and a clay and cobble podium faced with large sandstone blocks (**49**). Fragments of sculpture, among them a life-sized horse's head and a relief depicting Venus looking into a mirror with an attendant beside her, suggest that the deity in the temple might have been either Venus or Epona, the Celtic horse goddess, or conceivably both together. To the west of the temple lay a large rectangular enclosure with rounded corners with an alcove set in one side and a wide entrance in another. The double walls of the enclosure are identical to the construction seen in theatres and arenas and suggests that they supported timber seating. If so, this enclosure may have been the focus for rituals or for theatrical performances connected with the temple, a common association in the Romano-Celtic world. It may even be that the goddess Epona was worshipped here through the parading, racing, or sacrifice of horses, although there is no archaeological evidence for such practices in this instance (**colour plate 11**).

The other known temples of Wroxeter, a possible example located south of the baths, almost directly opposite the classical temple just discussed, and another which lay to the north of the modern farm buildings, were both Romano-Celtic in style. Such temples

49 *The classical-style temple (Site V on **42**), found by Bushe-Fox in 1913, under excavation. The large facing stones of the podium are still in place on one side but much of the temple has been robbed away*

can be readily identified from their concentric square or circular plans set within a larger sacred enclosure (*temenos*). Temples of this design are known in rural and urban contexts throughout the western Empire and are exactly what one would expect to see in a city of Wroxeter's size. Since neither has been excavated the deities worshipped in them are unknown. However, somewhere within the city there was a temple or shrine dedicated to a healing deity associated with eye troubles since within the debris brought in for constructing rubble platforms on the site of the baths basilica in the sub-Roman period were a number of votive replica eyes carved out of painted plaster. These were augmented by other examples, found on the same site, made of sheet metal, both bronze and gold, which would originally have been nailed to statues or boards. Their presence suggests a cult of sympathetic magic to cure eye diseases within the city, attested independently by the discovery of oculists' eye-ointment stamps.

Also found in the same rubble platforms was evidence for an even more bizarre religious cult. Several fragments of human skull, and one piece of animal skull, possibly from a horse or cow, were found. These had been treated with a natural vegetable oil after the skulls had been defleshed – one of the skulls showed distinct signs of scalping and another appeared to have been placed for a length of time on a bronze platter, staining its base green. The cult reminds one of the stories of Celtic head-hunting recorded by Diodorus Siculus who tells of the preservation by the Celts of human skulls in cedar oil, and also reminds us that ancient religious practices were not always benign. It should be pointed out, however, that it is highly unlikely that these skulls were

50 *Fragments from a carved capital found in the forum. It is decorated with three male heads carved in Celtic-style with lentoid eyes and symmetrical curly locks of hair. A fourth detached head was found nearby. The overall size, decoration, and function of this unusual capital is not known*

collected during the Roman period: human sacrifice was forbidden by Roman law and it may well be that these skulls were totems or even ancestors surviving from earlier tribal shrines located away from Wroxeter which had then been brought into the city. The importance of the head-cult at Wroxeter may also account for the curious fragmentary column capital decorated with male heads found on the forum site (**50**).

The last and perhaps most important aspects of religious life in the city were the rites surrounding the death and burial of its citizens. Unfortunately, little is yet known on the subject since there has been hardly any work carried out on the city's cemeteries. Roman law dictated that burials had to take place outside the city's limits and the site of Wroxeter's principal cemetery is known to have been located beyond the north-eastern, Watling Street, gate with cremations and tombstones having been found on both sides of the road. Cremations are known also at the north gate and to the east and south of the city. A grand mausoleum is hinted at by the eighteenth century discovery of a stone-built platform containing a glass urn with ashes and other goods found at the confluence of the river Tern and Severn a quarter of a mile to the north-west of the city. Fragments of the roof of this mausoleum with its scale-leaf pattern are built into the walls of Atcham church, the next village due west of Wroxeter, though the mausoleum may have belonged not to the city but to a suburban villa.

In addition to providing the city's main buildings, the city council was also required to provide its infrastructure: the grid of roads carrying people through and around the city's buildings; its water supply; and lastly, but most importantly, defining the limits of the city through the construction of its defences, separating the living from the dead and urban life from its rural counterpart. The defensive role of the city's defences was secondary to its civic one – ultimately the city's defence was provided by the Roman army stationed around the periphery of the province and the walls of Wroxeter were never conceived as structures to be defended, although they did of course prevent unauthorised entry to the city. Instead, they were designed to impress the visitor with their size and to force people to enter the city through its gates so that they would have to pay tolls on goods or livestock they were bringing in.

Many cuttings have been made through the city's defences and in addition, much has been learnt about them from aerial photographs. From this information, previous excavators have concluded that the city was defended by a bank and ditch system crowned by a stone wall, despite the fact that not one piece of stone or rubble or mortar has been found in the city ditch. It seems clear, rather, that the city defences were made solely of earth, cobbles and turf with a timber palisade and fighting platform, the normal construction used by the Roman army (**51**). The precise form of the defences is similar in many respects to that of the fortress. The core of the rampart, which lay 2m from the inner edge of the city ditch, consisted of a clay and cobble dwarf wall 2m wide and about 1m high. This dwarf wall would have supported a timber framework which projected above the rampart to form the palisade. Once this was in place, the rest of the rampart was formed from dumped soil excavated from the two V-shaped city ditches each 8m wide lying parallel to the rampart. The 2m wide gap between the clay wall and the lip of the inner ditch was filled with a sloping turf wall with dumped earth behind so that the ditch and sloping rampart together formed a continuous slope, a *glacis*. Thus the full height of the rampart, from the base of the inner ditch to the top of the rampart, was 11 metres. Behind the clay and cobble wall-core the rampart had a broader, gentler slope

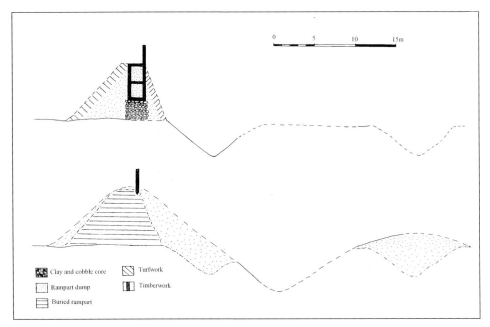

0   5   10   15m

Clay and cobble core   Turfwork

Rampart dump   Timberwork

Buried rampart

51 *Reconstructed cross-sections of Wroxeter's defences showing the early and late phases*

and was revetted at the back by a 1m high turf wall. The full width of the rampart was thus 10–15m. Gates were provided for all the roads entering the city with the most important, the Watling Street gate being perhaps being of stone, although the evidence for this is slight. The rampart has been traced around the whole of the periphery of the city, including the riverside on the west where there must have been postern gates to allow access from the harbour facilities which, it may be surmised, lay at the foot of the river cliff. Wroxeter's defences were thus formidable enough to provide an adequate barrier to those trying to enter the city and yet their closest parallel remains the defences known from the many hillforts around Wroxeter rather than the stone-built walls seen in the other cities of Roman Britain.

The water supply to a city the size of Wroxeter was of crucial importance and the course of Wroxeter's aqueduct is known in some detail even though the last remnants of it were sadly bulldozed and ploughed out in the 1950s (**52**). Aqueducts immediately conjure up an image of huge stone arches like those that survive at the Pont du Gard in France or at Seville in Spain. Wroxeter's aqueduct was nothing like these but was a clay-lined V-shaped channel or leat such as has been found in other cities in the northern provinces. The best preserved example in Britain is that at Dorchester (Dorset), which provides an exact parallel for Wroxeter's aqueduct. The water here came from a reservoir created by damming the Bell Brook at a point one mile east of the city, north of Beslow. The leat followed the contour of the valley, crossing the rampart just north of the city's east gate and close to the putative cattle market. It has been calculated that the channel was capable of delivering between 1.93 million gallons of water per day if filled to 1ft (300mm) depth, or 610,000 gallons if filled to 3in (75mm) depth, the water emptying into a settling and distribution tank, the *castellum divisorum*. From there, the

52 *A photograph of Wroxeter's aqueduct showing the channel before its destruction in the 1950s*

water would have been piped by gravity to all parts of the city, with the probable exception of the area to the north of the Bell Brook. The principal recipient must have been the city baths with pipes carrying the water into the building to fill the plunge pools and basins and supply steam, the overflow then being directed through the city latrines to flush them before passing into a deep drain to the south of the forum and thence to discharge into the river. Enclosed water pipes have been found running alongside some of Wroxeter's streets but the most remarkable feature of this type was a timber-lined drinking-water fountain found by the roadside adjacent to the north portico of the baths basilica, which may originally have been flush with the street surface (**colour plate 12**). Bushe-Fox found evidence for another type of water supply in which water flowed along open channels with sluices which allowed the water flow to be directed into some of the wealthier houses to flush latrines and supply private bath houses. Both systems testify to a considerable degree of civic engineering skill and these services would have been paid for by the fees charged for their use. The poorer inhabitants will have to have relied upon public fountains or on wells dug by themselves on their own land. Many of these have been discovered and must have provided the main sources of water, the water table at Wroxeter being high enough even today to supply a well still in use near the village.

The city's streets have been only partially examined although the basic grid is known from the extensive surveys which have been carried out. Originally the main streets seem to have been 10m wide with crushed red sandstone footings and gravelled surfaces. These broad streets were cambered and provided with roadside ditches or, along the more prestigious buildings and streets, open stone gutters. As their surfaces wore out, so new layers of gravel were placed over the old, leading to a gradual rise in levels. Narrowing of the thoroughfare was common, with buildings often encroaching onto the valuable street edges. The grid had different orientations: the area of the former fortress formed the core of the city and this still had a regular layout but the orientation of the grid along the Bell Brook valley was altered on both banks of the stream to take account of its curving course and this in turn led to blocks of irregular size where the two grid alignments met. Elsewhere, some adaptations were made to the grid as the city expanded to its periphery. Additional lanes were added within the more extensively-used *insulae* to allow owners access to the backs of properties and to gain access to smaller dwellings erected away from the street frontage or to gardens and working areas. There is also evidence that zoning of activities within the city also took place, with an area of metalworking being identified by Bushe-Fox, and kilns or working hearths being located in the eastern and north-western part of the city south of the Bell Brook. To the north of the brook, the market gardens alluded to in chapter 3 may have continued in existence whilst other areas seem to have been dedicated solely to residential housing. Such zoning is known in other cities, most comprehensively in Pompeii, where the evidence is naturally much clearer, and argues strongly for a well-developed and methodical city council which was able to plan and organise the space within the city's walls. The zone of potters' kilns also extended outside the city walls on its north-western side as is demonstrated by the discovery of the later second-century *mortarium* kiln here and by the presence of the tileries identified on the flood plain of the Severn near Ismore Coppice. The products of these latter kilns were almost certainly intended for the public buildings as a trackway still exists leading from their site up the river cliff to join a street running south of the forum and baths *insulae*. Thus the products of these kilns could be taken by cart straight from their place of manufacture to the building site.

Also at the foot of the river cliff, although unfortunately uninvestigated, may be the remains of Wroxeter's quays. These may lie in the marshy land adjacent to the island or bylet created in the Severn in the Middle Ages to position fish weirs or, alternatively, could lie by the ford at the southern end of the city. There is likely to have been provision for the loading and unloading of goods on quays or jetties here since the traffic on the river could have been considerable. A possible trackway from the marshy area close to the bylet passes obliquely up the river cliff to enter the city perhaps by a postern gate north of the large modern house standing on the river cliff. At the ford itself, there may have been a bridge. The squared stone blocks and timber found here in the past, and which can still be seen on the river bed, must represent the remains of medieval or later fish weirs. All trace of caissons or a superstructure of a Roman bridge will have long been washed away and it may well be that the ford was used without any bridge at all. Within the city, however, bridges must have existed on the sites of, or close by, the existing ones on the Bell Brook where the major thoroughfares cross this small stream.

6 The Late Roman city

Cities are never static. Every day it is possible to walk through a city and notice new buildings being constructed, or old ones torn down. Existing buildings are continually modified to reflect changes in society and in use. Wroxeter was in this respect no different from any other city and the late Roman cityscape was quite different from its earlier counterpart. Indeed, in remembering this, it is easy to forget for how long Wroxeter, and Britain itself, was occupied by the Romans. The fact that Britain was a Roman province for more than 350 years does not register until one remembers that the same period of time spans the death of the first Queen Elizabeth and the accession of the second. In the case of Wroxeter the Roman way of life continued even longer – for nearly 600 years, or equivalent to the period from the Peasants' Revolt of 1381 to the Poll Tax riots of 1987. With this in mind, it is not difficult to realise just how much society, and the Roman Empire itself, must have changed. Wroxeter was of course not immune to these changes and it too altered radically in the way that its people lived, their relations with the rest of the province, their government at both local and provincial level, and not least in their religion. These changes, though profound, were gradual and it is unlikely that those within the city will have been aware of the different life styles of their remoter ancestors.

Administratively, the city changed both in status and in its relationship to the rest of the province. Empire-wide reorganisations increased the numbers of provinces within Britain from two in the early third century to four in the fourth century. At the same time, the taxation system was reorganised so that assessments were made on an individual's land holdings for both area and value (based on their quality). Further, a poll tax was levied on the heads of households, both systems being underpinned by regular census. These changes had profound effects on local government as increasingly the burden of tax fell inequitably on the poorer city councillors (*curiales*) and the urban and rural poor since the wealthiest citizens often belonged to the senatorial class, which was exempt from taxation. Shortfalls in tax were still chargeable to the councillors and the state attempted to make sure that these were made good by appointing officials such as the *exactor civitates*, although such interventions were strongly resisted and were ultimately unsuccessful. As local government became a heavier and heavier burden so city councillors sought to avoid their duties, a move which the state attempted to counter by making the office of city councillor hereditary. More serious for the fabric of the city was the seizure by central government of an increasing proportion of the locally collected taxes. At times in the fourth century, this confiscation could be total and had obvious implications for the continued maintenance of a city's public buildings and infrastructure.

Wroxeter itself is likely to have changed in status too. In Ptolemy's Geography the city is referred to as *Viroconium Cornoviorum* but in the *Antonine Itinerary* (i.e. one of a number of road lists compiled for travellers) Wroxeter is usually referred to simply as *Uriconium*. Although this could just be a combination of scribal error and laziness, the name change might reflect both the later Roman pronunciation of the city's name and its elevation from a tribal capital to a chartered city, a *municipium*. Such a change in status would be a perfectly normal progression and one which would be largely academic in any case after the *constitutio Antoniniana* of 212 had made all free people living in the Empire into citizens. In practice, Wroxeter's elevation to chartered city status will have had little effect on its citizens being merely an administrative change to emphasise the continued pre-eminence of the city within the tribal area.

The other major changes in later Roman society which may have had an impact on Wroxeter's inhabitants and its rulers will have been the reorganisation of the army and widespread changes in the nature of religion. The role of the army within Wroxeter had for centuries been minimal and there will have been little change in this policy since the territory had been pacified for centuries and was so far from the sea that it was unlikely to be under threat of a raid. Nonetheless, there is little doubt that young men still enlisted in the army from the area since a *cohors I Cornoviorum* is recorded in a late Roman document, the *Notitia Dignitatum*, as being stationed at Newcastle on Hadrian's Wall sometime during the fourth century, the only known instance of British troops being posted within their own island. Of more direct relevance were other changes in the taxation system which saw the reorganisation of a tax in kind (*annona militaris*), levied specifically for the army to prevent inflation from biting into the resources to run the army efficiently. For the *Cornovii*, the *annona* may have been a serious burden since the presence of Chester within the tribal territory possibly meant that their tax had to be taken to the fortress at their own cost. The levy will have gathered food for both animals and men and will have provided clothing and other essentials. The only mitigation may have been that reorganisation of the army undoubtedly meant that there were fewer soldiers actually living in Chester's fortress since the reforms of the army seem to have reduced the strength of each legion from about 5500 to probably nearer 1000 men. At certain times, the levy in goods could be commuted into cash payments and certainly by the end of the fourth century this became more normal once confidence in coinage had resumed. Towards the end of the fourth century, the legion defending Chester, possibly still *legio XX Valeria Victrix*, was withdrawn. This may have occurred in 383 when the usurper Magnus Maximus raised the standard of revolt since this roughly coincides with the date of the latest-known coins from Chester. With the demise of the protection afforded by the army, the *Cornovii* may increasingly have felt threatened by attacks from the north by the Irish or Picts, and certainly by the mid-fifth century will have been aware of the Anglo-Saxon settlement of the south and east. Early in the century, the Emperor Honorius told British cities to look to their own defence.

Two remedies seem to have been taken by the *Cornovii* to protect themselves. One was to increase the strength of the city's defences and the second was to employ a small

53 *Martiobarbuli found on the baths basilica site. These late Roman lead-weighted darts were carried on shields by soldiers and used as anti-cavalry devices*

force of troops within the city. The strengthening of Wroxeter's defences seems to have taken place within the fourth century, in line with other towns and cities within the province, and may perhaps therefore have had more to do with prestige than with any perceived defence weakness. This is reflected in the fact that there is still no evidence even in this late phase for the adoption of stone fortifications. Rather, the ditches in front of the existing rampart were recut so that a single broad ditch was created, the spoil being dumped partly on the original rampart to heighten it and also on the outer lip of the ditch to create a raised bank (a counterscarp). The effect was to make the ditch higher at the lip and deeper so that the overall depth was increased considerably (see **51**). It has been suggested by Dr Arnold Baker that these measures were taken so that projecting bastions supporting artillery such as catapults and crossbows could be added at the front of the rampart. Bastions would also explain the modifications to the ditch since for such weapons to be effective the ditch had to be increased in depth and width to keep attackers in range. A suggested bastion site was excavated in the 1990s but turned out instead to be a gap in the foundation trench for the rampart where a natural plug of clay had been used by those building the city wall as a solid foundation for the rampart itself. Over time, the rampart material had been entirely ploughed away here exposing the gap in the rampart which looked like a bastion. Overall, therefore, there is still no definite evidence for the use of bastions on the city defences.

The refurbishment of the defences may be accounted for in a certain measure by competition between cities, but the evidence for late Roman soldiers within Wroxeter shows that there were serious concerns about security. The evidence for a military

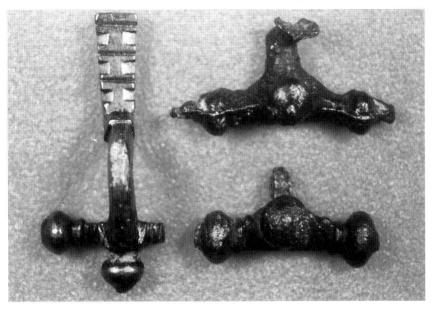

54 *Late Roman brooches from Wroxeter. Above is a complete fourth-century crossbow brooch with, beside it, two locally-produced variants dating probably to the early fifth century. One shows traces of 'flashing' – excess metal which has flowed into the joins in a mould. These flaws would be filed off later, as can be seen in the second example. Below are various penannular brooches (i.e. a ring with a gap in it through which a moveable pin can be passed) in bronze (top) or iron (below). These would have been locally produced*

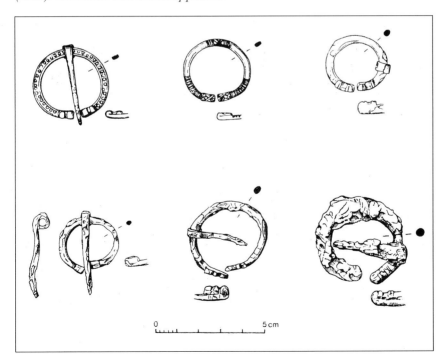

presence rests on the discovery in the latest layers on the baths basilica site of several lead-weighted darts, known to the Romans as *plumbata* or *Martiobarbuli*, Mars' darts (**53**). According to the late Roman military authority, Vegetius, five of these darts were carried behind the shield by each soldier and were used to inflict flesh wounds on opposing troops or their horses. Reconstructions have shown that they were probably thrown underarm, holding the flighted end so that they would rise and then plummet suddenly from a height, the barbs sticking cruelly into exposed flesh. Six examples were found in excavation and a further two have been found outside the city by metal detectorists. This is the largest known number from a single site in Britain and for a civilian establishment remote from the frontiers argues strongly for the presence of a military force stationed at Wroxeter. Further evidence for this may be adduced by the presence of crossbow brooches, several types of which have been found at Wroxeter, ranging in date from the late third to early fifth century (**54**). Traditionally these were worn by soldiers to pin their military cloaks but were also used by anyone employed by the state, including its civil servants. Such brooches are usually associated with the *cingulum militare*, military belt sets, which were also used as badges of office in the late Empire, a single example of which has been found in the city. We know nothing of the size and composition of this putative military force but the group is unlikely to have been large in number. There is a possibility that one of its later commanders could have been an Irishman, Cunorix, whose tombstone was ploughed up on the eastern rampart of the city in 1968 (**colour plate 13**). His epitaph consists solely of his name, which translates as Hound-King, and his tribal origin, 'son of the son of The Holly'. It is written in Latin letters but with an Irish spelling. Although there is no reference in the epitaph to his profession, if he had been a cleric or even a Christian, this would probably have been mentioned as in so many contemporary tombstones from elsewhere, and a military role seems the most likely reason for his presence in the city. If Cunorix was indeed a military commander we do not know whether he was in the employ of those still running the city, be it the city council, a 'tyrant', or its bishop. Possibly he was himself acting as *de facto* ruler of the city. If so, there is no evidence from his epitaph that this was the case.

The radical developments in late Roman society extended to religion too. Initially the change from pagan to Christian life had less profound effects but must have seemed somewhat perplexing at first to many people. After the persecutions of the third and early fourth century, Christianity found favour with Constantine the Great and his successors, with the notorious exception of Julian I (360–3). Throughout the fourth century, the Emperors increasingly promoted the interests of Christians at the expense of the established pagan religion but often these efforts were undermined by numerous schisms and controversies. Perhaps because of this, there is little evidence for Christianity at Wroxeter. Indeed the only piece of evidence adduced so far may be dismissed out of hand. This was a crude lead tablet found in the sacred spring at Bath on which was scratched a text translated in the 1900s to read as a letter from 'Visinius' to 'Niger' concerning a Christian community at Wroxeter. The recent decipherment of the complete corpus of Bath curse tablets by Roger Tomlin has shown that the original translator was reading the text upside down and when correctly transliterated the letter bears no reference either to Wroxeter or Christians.

Perhaps of more obvious relevance is a small coin, minted in 327 at Constantinople, which was found on the baths basilica site (**55**). This shows the *labarum* (battle standard)

55 *A coin of Constantine I, minted in 327. On the obverse is the head of the emperor and his titles, on the reverse the* labarum *piercing a snake. Written on either side is the legend SPES PUBLICA – The Hope of the Public [rests in the Emperor's rule]. Below is the mint mark of Constantinople. Enlarged x4*

decorated with Christ's monogram, the *chi-rho*, piercing a snake. The latter is often taken as an allusion to the pagan Emperor Licinius, a rival of Constantine's who was defeated by him in 324. The discovery of this rare coin at Wroxeter may hint at an early Christian presence there but coins are such portable objects that little weight can be placed on this suggestion. However, images like this, along with those on other coins, such as the very common issues of the House of Valentinian (364–38) which show the emperor standing holding a *labarum*, no doubt familiarised the population with the new religion and its iconography.

Wroxeter, isolated as it was from the principal ports of entry and away from the army centres, may have only slowly acquired a Christian community. Nonetheless, there is some evidence that once established, the new religion prospered in the city. Perhaps the clearest proof of Wroxeter's Christianisation comes from the demise of its temples which excavation has shown were abandoned within the fourth century and were despoiled. Even more intriguingly, a possible early Christian congregational church has been detected within the city centre (**colour plate 14**). The building appears on the geophysical surveys as a modest rectangular structure 30m long and 13m wide, orientated east–west and with an apsidal end. It is set back slightly from the street intersection and there is a portico on the west and north sides so that the building stands alone within an enclosed area. Internally the floor shows as a solid block suggesting a concrete or perhaps mosaic floor and there are stub walls defining two square rooms at the east end indicating that the building had a wide nave with aisles to the north and south. Fortunately this plan, which contradicts the current interpretation of the building on aerial photographic plots, was confirmed in the year of the survey by the parchmarks created in the exceptionally dry summer of 1995. The radar survey of the same area also showed that it was the latest identifiable structure on the site (see **37**). Buildings of this plan were used only for a limited number of purposes in the Empire. Their shape implies their use by those wishing to meet together either as a religious sect, such as Christians, Jews or worshippers of Mithras or as the members of a secular trade guild, a *schola*. Although the building could be a *mithraeum* of the sort famously excavated in London in the 1950s this seems unlikely since the buildings of this cult require a sunken floor to imitate the cave inhabited by their god. Additionally, *mithraea* often have a large pit close by the doorway where the *taurobolium* (ceremonial baptism in bull's blood) could take place. A feature like this should have been seen in the surveys. A synagogue is an even more improbable interpretation as the presence of Jews is barely attested in Britain, which leaves either a church or a secular *schola* meeting hall as the most probable interpretation. Ultimately only excavation can provide an answer to the role of this building but its presence certainly alerts us to the possibility that it might be the church of a community based within the city. Its prominent position, on the corner of a major road and on a neighbouring city-block to the public baths, also suggests it was built with the official sanction of the city council. If so, this too would square with the importance of Christianity within late Roman cities, and with the active promotion of the new religion by the state. Nonetheless, despite the official sanction of the new religion, the size of the church hints that the Christian community may have initially been quite a small proportion of the city's population.

The social impact of the religious transformation is also reflected in the changing fashion for dealing with death in society which saw a move from cremation of the deceased to inhumation in an organised and regulated cemetery. Although often linked to the rise in Christianity, this trend had arisen within the third century, before Christianity had become a mass religion, and it seems likely instead that the rite should be seen as one associated with the god *Sol Invictus* – the Unconquered Sun – who was particularly important in the third century. No late Roman graveyard has yet been excavated at Wroxeter but there is a distinctive cropmark beyond the north-west corner of the city which may be interpreted as an enclosed cemetery containing regular rows of graves. Parallels with cemeteries in other cities, for example Butt Road, Colchester and Poundbury, Dorchester (Dorset), indicate that such cemeteries might hold many hundreds of individuals, some in impressive *mausolea* which might in themselves form the focus of worship as *martyrium* churches. However, no hint of such structures has been detected around Wroxeter either in aerial photographs or fieldsurvey.

Wroxeter's new church, if such it was, was not the only alteration within the cityscape. The subtle changes in society also had their impact in the decline and demise of some of its public buildings, such as the forum and temples, and perhaps also in the increasing differences in wealth in society as manifested by the private dwellings in the city. Those who were wealthy were able to invest considerable sums in building projects, the clearest examples of this conspicuous consumption being the refurbishments of city houses alluded to in chapter 5 for example when the red sandstone house excavated in 1952–3 was rebuilt in grey Hoar Edge Grit with an additional summer dining room. Similar expenditure must also have been made on the surely magnificent city house represented by a mosaic found in Wroxeter village in 1827 (**colour plate 15**). This fragmentary floor can be reconstructed to a full dimension of at least 5m by 6m. The pattern, which is entirely geometric and dates to the third quarter of the fourth century, is virtually identical to the mosaic found in the principal room at Yarchester villa which lies 7 miles (11km) to the south-east of Wroxeter at the foot of Wenlock Edge, and also matches a more complete example found at Dyer Street, Cirencester. This latter example is one of several in this style, known as the Corinian Saltire School, found in

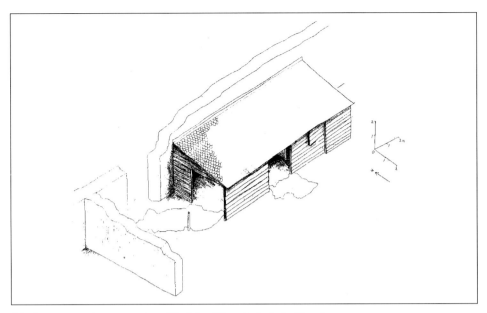

56 *An axonometric reconstruction of Building 23 on the baths basilica site*

Cirencester and its region, and there seems little doubt that the mosaicists who created floors in this style were based in or near Cirencester. Other mosaic pavements from Wroxeter may also be of this date but are too poorly recorded for further comment, although the patterned border from one example suggests similar opulence elsewhere. Such buildings may be contrasted with Wroxeter's more humble dwellings, of which we have no clear picture other than those on the baths basilica site (**56**). Inevitably, these humbler dwellings though less visible will have been far more numerous than the easily identifiable stone-built houses of the city and it is likely that Wroxeter, in keeping with other cities of the Empire, had abundant urban poor, giving an ever-increasing importance to the charitable functions of the Christian church, a function recognised in 321 when Constantine I made donations to the church legal.

The increasing polarisation of society extended also to Wroxeter's hinterland. Although many farms will have continued in use throughout the Roman period, we know that elsewhere in the Empire, and probably among the *Cornovii* too, poorer farmers became even worse off and in debt to their landlords. Consequently the rich were able to buy up more and more properties to create large estates which might be maintained by bailiffs on the landowner's behalf. The very rich might own properties in several provinces. The aristocrat Melania, for example, who came from an ancient Roman senatorial family, held estates in Italy, Sicily, Africa, Numidia, Mauritania, Spain, and Britain, whilst we know of city councillors in the Greek-speaking east who held several farms, not all in their own city's territory. Ownership of individual villas is impossible to prove in the absence of written records but absentee landlords were a common phenomenon. The very large estates are difficult to demonstrate archaeologically but their presence has been suggested in areas of southern Britain where sheep ranching for wool production would have been a very profitable enterprise.

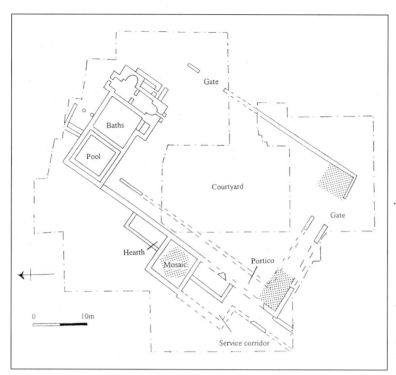

57 *A simplified plan of Whitley Grange Roman villa. The areas occupied by sub-Roman buildings are toned*

Whether such estates were formed in Cornovian territory is unknown and certainly the small number of villas around Wroxeter suggests limited development. This may perhaps be because the wealthiest Cornovians chose not to live near Wroxeter but instead had their country seats near the provincial capital, Cirencester, where they might have more influence. In such cases, their farms in Cornovian territory may have been run by bailiffs. The lesser ranks of aristocracy will have continued to live in the area and the little that we do know about Shropshire's villas indicates that the fourth century saw extensive redevelopment or even fresh construction in the countryside around Wroxeter. Excavations on the more lowly enclosed farmsteads, such as that at Sharpstones Hill on the fringe of Shrewsbury, have shown that houses were increasingly being built in Roman fashion as modest rectangular structures, some with tiled roofs.

Given our rather poor understanding of later Roman villas in Wroxeter's hinterland, it is unfortunate that the only villa to have been comprehensively excavated in Shropshire, Whitley Grange, does not conform to the usual picture of the villa as a Roman farm. Here, excavations uncovered a courtyard 60m by 20m with a baths suite on the north side and three rooms on the west side, both rooms and baths situated behind a colonnade (**57**). The baths consisted of two large rooms, one probably an indoor pool and the other an undressing room, and three heated rooms. A lean-to latrine was provided on the north side, downslope of the baths. The west wing consisted of a large square central room flanked by rectangular rooms on either side. This was clearly the most important room in the complex since it was paved with a splendid mosaic whose only parallel is from a villa in Warwickshire (**colour plate 16**). Behind the south-west side of the villa was a corridor which led to further (unexcavated) buildings.

58 *A photograph showing two of the mosaic panels in the north aisle of the baths basilica which have collapsed into a subsidence in the floor. This must have happened suddenly since there is otherwise little damage to the panels, suggesting they were covered over almost immediately to level the floor again*

All in all this was a sumptuous building, with its very large bath house and lavish mosaic, but by no stretch of the imagination can it be called a farm. Two possible uses for the building can be suggested. One is that it was some sort of religious complex, a pagan temple where one could wash to be purified and then worship in the associated cult room, or even have a ritual meal. If so, there were no finds to indicate what rites took place as few objects were found on the site. Perhaps more probable is that it was a 'holiday cottage'. The wealthy owner of the site could ride out from Wroxeter, on horseback, and perhaps spend time with friends hunting and fishing, the Rea Brook being only yards away from the site. The relative isolation of the site, in its wooded valley, visible but difficult to approach from the main Roman road which runs along the other bank, meant that those who passed by could see it but not bother the occupants. Such buildings hint at a luxurious lifestyle indeed for the upper echelon of society. The lack of accommodation at Whitley suggests that its owner lived either at Wroxeter or on a rural estate elsewhere. Other villas are also known in the hinterland of Wroxeter. Yarchester, which seems to be roughly contemporary with Whitley, has already been mentioned due its fine late fourth-century mosaic while others are known at Cruckton and Lea Cross, both in the same valley as Whitley. More are thought to exist elsewhere in the county but until these buildings are investigated it is uncertain what dates they were or what were their social or economic context.

Whilst those who were able to spent their money on private houses, they seem to have been less willing to spend it on maintaining the public buildings. In any case, public revenues designed for just such purposes were often seized by central government so that there were insufficient resources for the task. Public policy decisions could also have radical effects, most notably in the destruction of the temples already mentioned, but generally the fate of public buildings was probably decided on a more *ad hoc* approach, as in the case of Wroxeter's forum. Excavation has shown that the forum basilica burnt down at the end of the third century or beginning of the fourth and seems to have been abandoned after this catastrophe, though the forum square and the west range by Watling Street seem to have remained in use. The fire may have extended to other parts of the city too; a large area to the north-east of the forum within the gradiometry survey shows a reversal of polarity from negative to positive readings, a phenomenon most likely to have been caused by fire. This being so, there is a likelihood, given the direction of the prevailing wind, that the fire spread from the forum to this residential area. Such problems were commonplace in ancient cities and do not necessarily reflect social upheaval any more than did the Great Fire of London in 1666. The forum had burnt down on a previous occasion in the late-second century but in that instance the fire had spread to the south and although residential houses were destroyed they were soon rebuilt. The later fire, however, seems to have been more conclusive since the basilica was not rebuilt and some of the destroyed city houses also seem to have been abandoned. The unwillingness to rebuild the forum basilica could merely reflect a lack of funds or perhaps the realisation on the part of the city council that due to Wroxeter's diminished role as an administrative capital a large forum basilica was no longer required.

A similar decline can also be detected in the baths. Here, the splendidly decorated baths basilica and the heated rooms had been undergoing a slow deterioration. The archaeological evidence for this lay largely in its successive floors but can be assumed for the rest of the complex. The floors showed signs of wearing out in places, especially around doorways. The fine mosaics, once loosened, would have unravelled quickly and in some places localised subsidence into underlying pits had caused the floors to become dangerous (**58**). These holes were soon filled in and the building continued in use but eventually must have looked so shabby that a full refurbishment was required. The radical solution adopted was to replace large areas of flooring with durable herringbone tiling. This was inserted as large patches at the doorways in the west and north doors in the basilica and along virtually the whole length of the south aisle (**colour plate 17**). An equally large area of flooring was also laid at the east end of the nave which was rather cheaply finished off with a timber step to mask the abrupt change of level between the original floor and the new patch. The resulting effect, however, was to create a raised area at the east end of the basilica not dissimilar to the tribunal at the south end of the forum basilica. Whether this was intentional or not is unknown. It may just have been an economy designed to limit the reflooring to areas where it was absolutely necessary. Alternatively, it may indicate that with the forum basilica now out of use the baths basilica now doubled as a forum basilica as well, or even that this was an area set aside for an altar to the goddess of bathing, *Fortuna Balnearis* or another deity. Further areas of herringbone flooring were laid in the vestibule of the eastern baths suite and, more extensively, in the public latrine and *macellum* courtyard and latrine. These latter floors

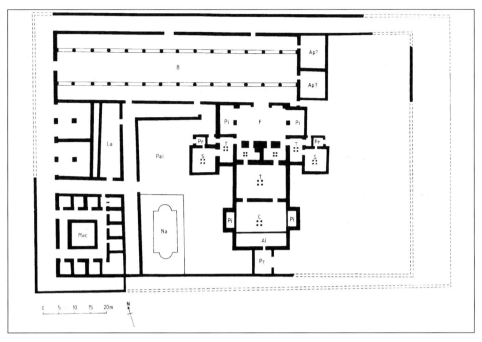

59 *Two plans of Wroxeter's public baths. That above shows the baths as originally constructed in 150 (the plan is at ground level and thus shows all known doors). That below gives one interpretation of what happened to the baths towards the end of their life (c.400). The main suites have been abandoned and demolished in favour of the side suites, leading to a reduction in the floor area and thus probably reducing the costs of running and maintaining the complex*

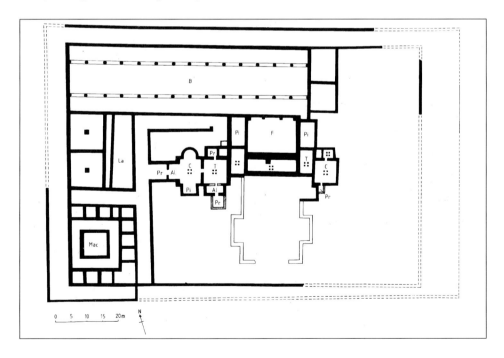

113

have produced the only dating evidence, a coin of Tetricus I (270–3) found in the foundations of the new floor. This gives an indication of the general period after which these repairs took place although this may be some time later. The scale of the repairs to the floors of the complex suggests extensive refurbishment of the rest of the buildings too. Certainly the roofs may also have been retiled. Roofs on buildings of this size had to be relaid every century or so, as the present maintenance programmes carried out on the country's cathedrals shows. Neglect of roofs would make the buildings eventually dangerous to use given their huge weight and it seems that the basilica's roof was relaid, the ceramic tiles being removed and replaced with large lozenge-shaped sandstone slates instead. These repairs suggest that civic funds were available for some projects and it is hardly surprising that the public baths were maintained in this way since baths were always popular. Improving their appearance and operation will have been a certain way to curry favour with the population.

Further extensive modifications detected in excavation were also made to the main heated baths suite, although this evidence is capable of several interpretations (**59**). For example, the ash dump from the main furnace which was excavated in the late 1960s had a sequence of pottery that ended in the late third or early fourth century. This would appear to indicate that the furnace went out of use at this time. This disuse may be associated with a new furnace built against the east wall of the warm room whose purpose could have been either to heat the warm room, directly to boost its heat level, or alternatively it could imply that the former warm room had become the new hot room and that the old hot room had been abandoned along with its furnace. This could have taken place either because the main rooms had structural problems, as is perhaps evidenced by the encasing wall built around them earlier, or that perhaps the cost of heating such large rooms had now become prohibitive. A further stage of deterioration is implied by the blocked doorways seen in photographs taken in 1859 of the wall between the *frigidarium* and the heated rooms (see **6**). Clearly, at some stage in the history of the baths, these doorways were blocked after the rooms beyond became unused, or unusable. Interestingly, the same photograph shows that the doors into the side suites remained open, as was confirmed by excavations in 1988 which showed extensive wear patterns leading to these doors. The impression given is that the main heated rooms were abandoned in favour of enlarged versions of the side suites which, being considerably smaller even after enlargement, would have been cheaper to heat in any case. Perhaps too the abandonment of the larger rooms of the baths reflected a decrease in the city's population. Even the side suites seem to have been further modified with additional furnaces being built against the western warm room and the eastern hot room. If the larger rooms of the main heated suite were indeed abandoned at this time, they would almost certainly have been dismantled almost immediately. Not only were the tiles in such buildings especially valuable for reuse in private buildings but the structures themselves would have had to be made safe so that they did not collapse, endangering the city's inhabitants.

The time-scale for these modifications and adaptations to the baths is wholly uncertain. They could have taken place relatively swiftly after the end of the third or the beginning of the fourth century but a slightly later time-scale can also be suggested on the basis of comparison with the sequence on the baths basilica. As already noted, the flooring of the basilica had been repaired with herringbone tiles in the late third or early fourth century, a date derived from the *macellum* floor. This was followed by a sequence of more ephemeral repairs which took place before a large-scale reflooring of the entire basilica, which was fortunately securely dated as after 367 by a coin of Gratian minted between 367–75. This comprehensive reflooring treated the basilica as an entity but did not provide it with a uniform floor surface. Rather, the materials chosen for the floors reflected the anticipated wear. The hardest surface, pebbles reinforced with stone boulders, was used in the most exposed area around the west doorway whilst hard mortar floors appeared at the east end of the nave and in the aisles. Between these harder surfaces the less frequented areas of the central nave had floors of beaten earth. These new floors in turn soon became quite worn and were first patched and then renewed overall twice more. The complicated wear patterns that evolved in the floor, and the obvious length of wear that some of the surfaces had been exposed to, led to the conclusion that each of these phases may have lasted thirty years or more. However, such estimates of wear can only be very approximate since they depend upon the overall amount of traffic and the footwear being worn, often, in Roman times, with studded soles. If there is a link between the date of the reflooring of the basilica and the date of the sequence of modifications to the baths, then it might be concluded that the main baths suite could have been abandoned in the later fourth century, resources instead being concentrated on refurbishing and improving the side suites and the basilica. It was also apparent from the excavations on the basilica that the work had been coordinated from the two-roomed annexe at the east end of the building. Here, there were abundant signs of a builders' yard with heaps of mortar, rubble and other materials gathered together so as to make running repairs to the buildings. Ramshackle structures leaning against the walls sheltered hearths, mixing areas and a barrel indicating that the roof, and eventually the dividing wall, had been taken away. These rooms were clearly being used throughout the whole phase and show that the baths were still in operation even at this late date.

The chequered history of the baths shows all too clearly the pressures in late Roman cities. After the building boom of the mid-second century, such buildings were beginning to show their age by the early to mid-fourth century. Large buildings need constant maintenance if they are to remain in use. Neglect will lead to their ruin, and can do so surprisingly rapidly, as is witnessed by the fate of the castles after their disuse. What despoilers do not take, the weather will destroy until the remains are buried. Since Wroxeter's large public buildings were all put up at roughly the same time, essential repairs will probably have been required nearly simultaneously, leading to painful decisions as to which building had precedence over another. Accidents like the destruction of the forum basilica by fire meant that the cost-cutting decision not to rebuild could be taken, the resources instead being used to refurbish the baths and city defences, for example. That refurbishment of the baths would have been popular with the citizens cannot be doubted – it was a lot more useful than the forum basilica and since there are no other known places of entertainment in the city, such as theatres or amphitheatres, its importance may have been magnified. To keep the baths in operation, however, cost-cutting measures were called for and thus the development and maintenance of the side suites at the expense of the large heated bath rooms made perfect sense. Furthermore, the baths basilica and *macellum* were good substitutes for the forum and meant that resources could be concentrated in one city block. Similarly, the refurbishment of the defences would have been popular too. No one relished the prospect of the city being attacked and since labour was cheap and plentiful and the use of wood kept costs down, the decision was a sensible use of scarce resources.

Despite the difficulties posed by inflation and polarisation in society, people will still have wanted to have shops in the city and there is little evidence for the decline of trade. Certainly, the stalls on the baths basilica portico seem to have continued in existence right through the fourth and fifth century, despite the fact that the currency is known to have collapsed by at least the early fifth century. In spite of this, trade continued, as it always does in non-monetary economies, with barter taking over. Payment in kind, perhaps as a form of tithes, may well also have replaced taxation – it had certainly done so in the later third and early fourth century when the *annona* became an important component of the tax regime and there is no reason why such a system could not have been reinstituted later on.

The decline of the money economy will, however, have had profound effects on some trades, particularly manufactured goods imported from elsewhere in Britain and the Empire. Certainly, archaeologists who have studied the quantity and range of manufactured goods can demonstrate diminishing trade through different styles and makes of pottery or glass, although it is less likely that people at the time noticed these subtle variations. The analysis of abundant manufactured goods such as pottery and glass tells us that by the later Empire the larger industries producing pottery abroad, such as samian ware, had collapsed in the mid-third century crises, the vacuum being filled by well-made derivative British products from Oxfordshire or the Nene Valley near Peterborough. The flourishing of these kilns emphasised the increasing self-reliance of the late Roman economy in Britain. Some wares, such as Dorset's Black Burnished industry, continued in production but were supplemented and eventually replaced by other cooking wares such as Shell-tempered ware, a relatively coarse and heavy product robust enough to survive cooking but hardly good enough for table ware. The Severn Valley production sites continued probably until late into the fourth century, as did most Romano-British potteries still in production at the beginning of that century, but eventually these pottery sources dried up to be replaced as in the Iron Age by metal, wooden and leather vessels. Clearly, the collapse of a money economy had a disproportionate effect on the pottery industry and it is clear that barter could be no replacement as a method of payment for such goods.

Throughout the third and fourth century glass formed an increasingly important element in the late Roman household at Wroxeter, these vessels being imported from the Rhineland. Indeed, the Rhenish trade in this late period seems to have been quite significant. It may have been based on the shipping of wine whose barrels, so visible on the grave monuments of Germany, tend not to survive, but equally could have been limited to the import of glass vessels and fine pottery, including motto-beakers. Along with such mundane artefacts came more exotic pieces, such as the Wroxeter mirror (**colour plate 18**). This splendid piece of late Roman silverware, nearly a foot in diameter and ornamented with an elaborate Hercules-knot handle, is perhaps to be dated to the later third century and was found in the forum excavation. It is of a type well-known from contemporary images, such as a grave relief from Neumagen in Germany showing a woman at her toilet, her servant holding the mirror in front of her. A painted panel from the coffered ceiling of the imperial palace at Trier shows another example in use, on this occasion held by a woman thought to be either Constantine the

Great's wife or sister (**colour plate 19**). She holds the large mirror awkwardly but the Hercules-knot handle is clearly visible. (Modern attempts to use the mirror like this have shown that it cannot be used in this way as its convex surface means it has to be held at greater than arm's length; the Neumagen relief shows the correct way to use such a mirror.) An object like this was destined for the wealthiest in Cornovian society.

Those who could not afford silverware for their tables could, however, use pewter. This alloy was a popular product in late Roman Britain since the required metals, namely lead and tin, were both to be found within the island. The decoration and shape of these vessels clearly imitates silverware and this probably reflects the wishes of those less well off to mimic the fashions and lifestyle of the rich. The discovery of the lower half of a stone mould for a deep pewter dish suggests strongly that pewterers were at work somewhere in the city. But eventually these products too ceased being imported into the city, presumably as an outcome of the collapse of the money economy, and substantial long-distance trade to Wroxeter seems to have ended.

For Wroxeter's craftsmen and tradesmen this cannot have been an easy period. Late Roman fashion tended not to indulge in brooches, other than those worn to pin cloaks. Beads and earrings were more common, if more delicate, than in the early Empire. Sometimes these could be in quite exotic materials, such as jet, amber and shale, the raw materials being imported into Wroxeter and perhaps worked there. Unfortunately, the precise impact of these changes cannot be measured without excavating Wroxeter's late Roman workshops, or its cemeteries where people may have been buried with their personal belongings. However, it is perhaps significant that bronze casting of late Roman crossbow brooches was still being practised at Wroxeter at the very end of the fourth or early in the fifth century as evidenced by the waste casting and a finished example of the brooch type, both excavated by Donald Atkinson on the forum site (see **54**). There seems also to have been a flourishing ironworking industry in the city into the latest Roman period, manifested in iron penannular brooches and iron writing *styli*, many of the latter being inlaid in silver. Other trades known to flourish in the late Roman city include bone-and antler-working, these materials being used for personal adornment and for furniture inlay. This industry was of course a by-product of what must still have been Wroxeter's most important industry, the trade in livestock and their products. There is little to show a decline in this trade throughout the late Roman period and the *annona* may well have encouraged livestock production so that taxes might be met in full.

7 The Dark Age town

The sources for the history of Britain between the fifth and the seventh centuries are scattered, varied, and ambiguous. Almost all, except for inscribed and carved stones, are later in date than the period in which we are interested, while those manuscripts that we have are mostly copies of copies, often corrupted in transmission. The three chief manuscript sources – *De Excidio Britonum* of the monk Gildas (used as a chief source by Bede in his *Ecclesiastical History of the English People*); the anonymous British Historical Miscellany (B.L. Harley 3859), often known as *Nennius* after its suggested compiler; and the earliest parts of the *Anglo-Saxon Chronicle* – all look back at, and reconstruct in various ways, history as they perceived it. Welsh poems, handed down orally, seem to describe events in western Britain in these early centuries, but there is now increasing doubt if they can be relied upon as evidence. More likely is that they reflect contemporary events in an anachronistic manner. Even if they reflect memories of long-distant battles and the exploits of heroes, they have been embroidered and transformed in the telling, and become increasingly ambiguous, so that it becomes impossible to separate fact from invention.

Inscriptions, almost entirely confined to tombstones, are a powerful witness to the Christian faith in western Britain and say much about individuals, their language and the survival of Roman forms of address, but little about the changing patterns of settlement, or defence, or the economy.

The diffuse picture that we have of post-Roman western Britain can be brought into sharper focus by archaeology, by both non-destructive fieldwork and by excavation. The history of the Cornovian area in sub- and post-Roman times is particularly obscure, but has been illuminated in the past quarter of a century by intensive excavation of the city centre of Wroxeter, by fieldwork initiated by the Wroxeter Hinterland Project, and by the work of historians such as Dr Steven Bassett and Dr Margaret Gelling. The most relevant excavated evidence has come from the site of the baths basilica. The methods used on this site enabled for the first time the identification of a series of timber buildings constructed in Roman style, and to a Roman system of measurement, but quite unlike the early timber-framed or masonry houses of the early city. During this period three major changes in activity were detected, each showing distinct patterns of use of the basilica or its site and attesting to continuing life within Wroxeter.

By the end of the fifth century the baths basilica and possibly parts of the baths themselves were still in use although apparently quite dilapidated. The last reflooring in the basilica shows this most clearly, consisting as it did of a surface of thin crushed tile in mortar laid upon a substantial dump of top-soil like material (commonly called 'dark earth' by archaeologists) which had all the appearance of rotted-down domestic refuse dumped here for want of anything more suitable as a foundation. Using the basilica by this time must have been a rather risky and unpleasant experience and it was no surprise that the next phase showed that the building had been closed to the public, although it still remained in use. The evidence for the closure came from the changed appearance of the porticoes and from the construction of a number of small, flimsy buildings within the basilica itself. The north and west porticoes were plainly sacrificed at this stage, the stone columns being removed along with most of the stone foundation-blocks, or stylobates, on which they had stood. At one point, near the annexe at the east end of the basilica, four stylobates were left in place as the foundation for a timber building – the post supports for the corners of this building lay at either end of the stylobates and had been held in place by fragments of the column bases themselves (**60**). A second, post-built, building stood adjacent to this on the east side whilst to the west was a small oven or furnace. Another two buildings were erected on the west portico, on either side of the main door of the basilica, the northern one containing a large oven and hearth, the latter proving to have quantities of burnt grain. Between the west portico and the buildings by the annexe the portico surface had become especially dangerous, not to say unusable, since there had been large-scale, deep subsidences of the floor into underlying pits. Those responsible for the maintenance of the basilica had dealt with the problem by planking the portico surface over to form a timber boardwalk – the positions of joists and even the drip-lines between planks were visible when first uncovered (**colour plate 20**). The presence of both buildings and boardwalks attests to the continued use of the porticoes, but obviously not in their previous form. Presumably the portico roof had become dangerous, and rather than risk life and limb, the authorities had dismantled it. Quite what they were kept open for is another matter. Perhaps stall-holders still occupied the porticoes, protected by a canvas awning, whilst at least one of the buildings appears to have been a bakery.

Inside the basilica, a number of lightweight and ephemeral buildings were put up. Three were simple wattle-built constructions at the east end of the north and south aisles and in the nave, but the most remarkable example was in the south-east corner of the basilica, between the annexe and the doorway into the *frigidarium* (still surviving in the Old Work). Here, the very floor of the aisle was quarried away entirely down to the underlying mortar foundation, a depth of about half a metre. The flooring materials were then perhaps reused elsewhere and the resulting quarry pit was partially built over by creating a lean-to in the corner where metal working seems to have been carried out. In the nave close by the annexe a shallow pit was dug and filled with burnt limestone, presumably so that it might be slaked. This seems never to have happened and instead the lime solidified into a solid concrete mass. While this mixture was still putty-like, however, a heavy weight was placed on it which was later removed, the resulting hollow being then used to melt lead. Quite what was going on here will never be clear but the evidence for building and maintenance is apparent. Within the annexe, where a maintenance crew was apparently based in the previous period, the buildings had been aban-

60 *A view of four surviving north portico stylobates on the baths basilica site. At a late date, the other stylobates were robbed out leaving these four. The columns that had stood on them were taken down and some of the bases were smashed, the pieces being used to pack a posthole adjacent to one of the stylobates (foreground). Another column base lies discarded behind. The evidence points to the stylobates being used as the foundation for a late timber building*

doned and an area of slaked lime had been spread out to dry. Elsewhere, a heap of rubble was piled as though for reuse. The maintenance team had apparently now left the annexe and expanded their activities into the basilica itself, a clear sign that the basilica could no longer be in public use. The team seems to be attempting to keep the baths in operation even though the basilica had been abandoned. Eventually, however, even they had to bow to the inevitable and at last the roof of the basilica was taken down and its internal columns removed.

Naturally, one might expect at this point that the shell of the basilica would have been demolished or left to fall down but instead, the basilica's interior was once again used by the general public. To achieve this the rough floor was levelled with a dump of dark earth covered by a discontinuous layer of roofing slates. Careful recording of the slates showed that they had been laid as an evenly-spread layer rather than the heap that might be expected from the collapse of a roof. Furthermore, the slates were densest around known doorways in the building although the doorways most in demand had rubble rather than slate paths laid leading from them. Where these rubble patches were found, it was observed that they had been exposed to considerable wear as their surfaces were evenly worn. The evidence is unequivocal: the basilica was once again in use but without its roof and, moreover, it was being used by a substantial number of people.

However, not all of the vast area of the basilica was equally used. By the Old Work, for example, the quarry hole of the previous period was filled first with a dozen pole-axed cattle skulls and then by a dump of rubble and midden-like dark earth which included within it a dispersed coin hoard of the mid-fourth century. The rubble remained unworn and this corner appears to have become derelict. At the other end of the south aisle, by contrast, a small building was erected in what must have been one of the more frequented parts of the basilica.

No direct evidence was found to tell us what was happening inside the basilica's shell at this late date but a clue was provided by the evidence of the former porticoes of the building. Here, curiously, and in contrast with the previous period, these areas appear to have been deserted. The bread oven and its building fell into disuse, the last date of its firing being given by a remanent magnetic date of between 490–550. (This dating technique measures the direction of magnetic north when the oven was last used; since magnetic north moves in a known pattern, its precise direction can tell us when it was last fired.) The inescapable conclusion is that the activity once carried out on the portico had moved into the basilica's shell so we should perhaps imagine that the many people thronging the basilica were visiting market stalls (**61**). Even though the lack of imported goods in this period makes it abundantly clear that external trade was becoming increasingly rare and fitful, people still had to eat and be clothed and so there would always have been a need for a market like this. By now too the money economy had long since collapsed and so whatever trade was going on in the basilica's shell must have been transacted through barter. The conversion of a public building in this way reminded one of the staff of the excavation, who now lives in Warsaw, of the principal black market in communist Warsaw, held in the ruins of a burnt-out government building which had not been reconstructed after the Second World War. Indeed, produce markets very similar to those we are suggesting are still held in some country towns in Britain, where a trestle table may be rented for the sale of surplus chickens, eggs, vegetables or jam, and an even more familiar parallel is provided by the now ubiquitous car boot sale.

Whether or not the former basilica was being used as a market cannot be proved, but whatever was going on there it is obvious that there was still an authority of some sort controlling the former public building since the decision to level the interior and lay paths clearly involved a degree of organisation, and a workforce to control. Similarly the structured filling of the quarry hole (first noisome refuse then a thick leveling dump of sterile earth and rubble to seal it) suggests that that authority was still concerned about public health. Unfortunately, we shall never know for sure who that authority was at this date but it may have been the rump of the town council trying to keep some sort of civic order in an increasingly deteriorating situation. Whatever the explanation, life in the city had clearly reached a low ebb. The only new buildings were small structures of unknown purpose at the west end of the basilican aisles and the latest of a series of bow-sided, wattle and daub industrial buildings outside the precinct to the east. The date span for this lowest period in the city's life is 500/550 – 530/580, with central dates of 525-550.

The next period of the town's history, starting around the mid-sixth century, shows such a dramatic change of use that it is tempting to see its genesis in a period of extreme social, political, and environmental instability. Perhaps the changes arose out of a combination of events, both natural and social. Recently, scientists working in other fields within the archaeological world have identified an important natural event whose

61 *A suggested reconstruction by Peter Scholefield of the ruined shell of the baths basilica in the early sixth century when it was perhaps being used as an open market. There is no evidence for the stalls shown here but we do know that the shell of the basilica was extensively used at this time from the patterns of wear detected on the site*

impact may have had just such profound social effects. The event, known as the 536-40 Event, was first identified by dendrochronologists, scientists who date timber through counting and matching tree-rings. Since each ring is unique in width and similar trees will respond in the same way to environmental conditions, broad environmental changes can be traced over wide areas using the technique. The dating sequence for Britain has largely been constructed by Prof. Mike Baillie who, in carrying out the work, noted that there were particular years that were especially poor for tree growth. One such period was the 536-40 Event. Tree-ring analysis shows such poor growth in this period that it must have been a time of intense cold, drought and darkness lasting from about AD 536 until probably as late as AD 545, with a dramatic plunge in the graph of tree-ring growth, indicating a year of extreme environmental stress, in AD 540.

Baillie was not alone in noting this phenomenon. Other scientists in other fields also saw evidence for the same event and have tried to explain it. For example, Clube and Napier in their book *The Cosmic Winter* put forward the theory that the earth entered a shower of space debris that would have produced spectacular phenomena in the sky – comets, meteorites and magnetic storms, perhaps accompanied by earthquakes, but more significantly, a dust-veil encircling at least the northern hemisphere. This will have screened-out the sun, causing gloom and increasing cold, phenomena that climaxed in 540, as the tree-rings testify.

At Wroxeter, it may be argued that these events had their effect since between AD 530 and 580 the city centre was transformed. Most of the remains of the basilica were swept away and the site leveled. In its place, and in the immediately adjoining *insulae*, a series of timber buildings, many of them massive, was constructed. Such wholesale changes surely mark a radical change in the social fabric of the town's inhabitants, a question that will be discussed further below. Before doing so, however, it is worthwhile outlining the archaeological evidence since, in the absence of written accounts, it is upon such information that we must base our understanding of the site's history.

To prepare the site, the basilica's north wall was demolished to ground level or lower and it is probable that the upper parts of the other walls were lowered to make them safe. The good-quality facing stones seem to have been retained for reuse elsewhere while the rubble core and smashed bonding tiles were set to one side. Possibly at the same time, or slightly earlier, the remaining stylobates in the north portico were taken away and a 30m stretch of the north street surface adjacent to it was dug out to a depth of up to 1m. Anyone who has had the misfortune to try to dig through a Roman road will realise what an enormous task this must have been. Extraordinarily, the spoil from this exercise was then sieved, the finer residue being systematically tipped back into the trench. The loss of bulk was made up by adding humus-rich earth, the final surface of the new street being left with a slight camber to allow drainage. Given an adequate task force these remarkable and unparalleled labours may only have taken a brief span of time. We do know, however, that the labourers for this project, and certainly for the great rebuilding that followed, used the adjacent north portico close by the annexe, where the north wall had been retained to at least head-height, as a cooking place. The evidence consisted of a considerable number of open hearths, many made from reused tiles and slates, built on top of rough dumps which had accumulated against the wall. As there was no sign of even the flimsiest of structures associated with these hearths it is assumed that people only cooked here. Certainly, the burnt food residues that were found with the hearths showed that they were eating rye bread, probably unleavened, a food considered fit only for labourers and peasants in the Roman period.

Once these preparations had been completed construction on the site of the basilica commenced with the laying out of platforms made from the heaps of demolition material that had been generated, with the addition of material from elsewhere in the city (**62**). As much as 250 cubic metres of material was used. The largest of these platforms, that for Building 10, had its central point opposite the middle doorway in the south wall, west of the Old Work, where a large column drum and an unfinished column capital were placed 11 Roman feet (3.24m) apart in the centre of the former nave, framing the doorway to the new building. These stones appear to have supported a columned porch since a narrow rectangular area behind them showed clear evidence from the underlying surface, which had untrampled animal bone lying on it, that the area had been planked over. Beyond this porch and verandah, and projecting either side to the south, was the rubble platform proper. This had been laid to take account of the slope of the site with the thickest edge on the south side and the high point at the north-east corner. The projecting wings of the platform at the south-east and south-west corners were especially carefully built, as was the façade. In these areas the rubble, broken into pieces of similar size, was laid in deliberate rows and then packed with plaster. On examination, this was found to have come from a curved ceiling and had a carpet-like pattern of laurel wreaths with central flowers above a red band. The use of freshly-broken rubble and plaster in this way shows that not only was the construction of the platform a deliberate and planned action,

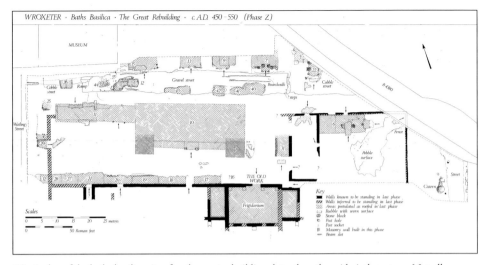

WROXETER · Baths Basilica · The Great Rebuilding · c.A.D. 450-550 (Phase Z)

62 *A plan of the baths basilica site after the great rebuilding, later than the mid-sixth century. Not all buildings are shown – in many areas there were a number of buildings built successively on the same sites. The gravel street is also shown with later buildings on it. As originally constructed it seems to have been empty of structures*

but also probably shows that the baths had finally fallen into disuse since a curved ceiling like this must have come from one of the nearby heated rooms.

The rubble platform laid out was of considerable size, stretching as it did across the full width of the north portico, north aisle and half the nave, a distance of 15.6m, with its northern and southern sides 33.5m apart. Together, these measurements represent nearly one half of an *actus* or Roman acre (35.4m²), and this shows that the platform was a planned action laid out by engineers trained in Roman fashion. It must surely have supported a massively-constructed timber-framed building since such a structure has no need of foundations other than a stable base. The depth of the platform and the care taken in its construction also suggests that the building was two-storied with projecting wings or towers, which themselves may have been two or even three storeys in height, flanking the entrance (**63**). It might be doubted that such a large building could have been constructed on such a foundation but this is similar to the sort of evidence that is uncovered when the sites of large, timber-framed houses of medieval date are excavated, a building tradition particularly strong in Shropshire. Such buildings derive their strength not from their foundations but from the jointing of the framing which ties the walls together, with additional bracing to prevent warping or twisting. What was even more intriguing about the building was its orientation. Rather than looking out onto the newly-created gravel street, it faced instead onto the blank south wall of the former baths basilica.

Flanking Building 10 were two buildings of differing construction. Building 31, to the east, was built from freshly-quarried yellow sandstone mortared to form a wall 3m high. Its length was uncertain but it could have extended across half the width of the nave and the north aisle, a distance of about 9m. Its west wall had later collapsed towards Building 10 and had been left where it fell. The western building, Building 11, was aligned east-west and joined the west wall of the former basilica to Building 10, a distance of 25m.

It had a mixed construction with low stone walls supporting timber-framing at the west end and posts holding wall panels at the east end. A staggered entrance lay between the two sections so that those passing through the building had to walk diagonally across its 5m width to get to the other doorway. There may have been a connecting door between Buildings 11 and 10 but this is by no means certain. Further ancillary buildings (17–21, 27 and 28) were detected on the former south aisle and especially to the west of the central doorway in the former basilica's south wall. Here, six regularly-sized building platforms were found, four measuring 8.3m in length (equal to 28 Roman feet), one of 8.6m (29 Roman feet) and one of 8m (27 Roman feet). The westernmost of these platforms had been unequally sub-divided to form two conjoined structures, Buildings 27 and 28, one of which had a hearth, but the others had no evidence for internal fittings or partitions and were of mixed construction using mainly timber-framing or wattles.

Yet more buildings associated with the complex were found east of the annexe, itself now completely deserted, in what had been the service area of the baths. Here there was a succession of buildings of either timber-framed or mixed construction, some leaning against the standing walls of the baths compound, others being free-standing. These structures were varied in size: the largest, Building 24, was a barn-like building 12m by 4m with a massively built porch, while Building 6, which was slightly smaller, was subdivided by a transverse passage giving it the appearance of a medieval long-house. None of these buildings had the appearance of being dwellings suggesting that they were storage buildings of some kind. It is also likely that the *frigidarium* of the baths should also be counted as being included within this complex of buildings since the only door into this room likely to have still been in use was that leading into the area in front of Building 10. What the *frigidarium* was now used for can only be guessed at although it is apparent that it can no longer have been associated with the baths since these were now ruinous. One possible clue comes from the dozen burials found by Thomas Wright within the hypocaust surrounding the *frigidarium*. Wright immediately leapt to the conclusion that these were poor wretches who had fled the (assumed) fire and sack of the town and had perished in the hypocaust from asphyxia or starvation. Despite the drama evoked by this picture, it is far more likely that these people had been deliberately buried here since it would be a simple matter to break through the raised floor of the heated rooms to bury a body rather than going to the effort of digging a grave. What is certain is that these burials demonstrate that Roman civic law had to some extent broken down as burial within the city walls was illegal in normal circumstances. This law had changed gradually under the impact of Christianity whose followers increasingly demanded burial near a place of worship, even if that lay within the city walls. This of course raises the possibility that the *frigidarium* had found a new function as a chapel or church. The room was orientated correctly east-west and, if enough of the decoration still survived, it would have been suitably grand for such a use. The reuse of public buildings, and especially bath houses, in this way was not at all uncommon since they were sturdily built and with their water supply and plunge pools made ideal locations for baptisms. The church of St Nicholas at Leicester, for example, was also built immediately above the unheated room of the public baths and even reused one of the walls of the room which now survives as the Jewry Wall.

If the *frigidarium* had indeed become Wroxeter's church then the likeliest occupant of Building 10, and for instigating the work in the first place, can perhaps be identified as a bishop. Such a conclusion may take some by surprise but in the context of the later and immediate post-Roman world this makes perfect sense. Bishoprics had been established by the emperors in the fourth century in every major town. Once established, they are likely to have become self-perpetuating, appointing and re-appointing among themselves since there was no authority to answer to other than the emperor, the pope not yet having established primacy in the west. This situation is more clearly seen in Gaul from the fifth-century writings of Sidonius Apollinaris and, in the sixth century, Gregory of Tours. These Gallic clerics also highlight another trait of the church at that time: both were prominent members of the local aristocracy and with little doubt the candidates for bishops were selected largely from the upper echelons of society, unless popular piety demanded otherwise, as in the case of St Martin of Tours. A British example of a local aristocrat who became prominent in the church is of course St Patrick, who tells us in his *Confessio* that his father had been a *decurion*, probably at Carlisle. Patrick was unusual, however, in not staying within his local region but instead choosing to minister to the Irish who had captured him as a boy. Bishops drawn from the local aristocracy would have had a vested interest in keeping towns functioning since without a congregation they would have no *raison d'être*. It would not be fair to say, however, that these men acted only from self-interest. It is clear above all from the letters of Sidonius Apollinaris, bishop of Auvergne at Clermont Ferrand at the end of the fifth century, that his prime concern was the spiritual and physical welfare of his flock, his fellow citizens. He pleaded, for instance, with the besieging Visigoths to spare both the town and its people, and also concerned himself with making sure that they had enough food to survive. In Rome the papacy was also gradually taking on the reins of power, including the honorary titles of High Priest (*Pontifex Maximus*) and City Prefect (*Praefectus Urbis*) as the eastern emperor's hold on the once great city declined leaving its inhabitants to fend for themselves. It would only be natural, therefore, if Wroxeter's bishop should take on the duties of maintaining the town's fabric for as long as possible. That he should at the same time house himself in a building commensurate with his new role and dignity is hardly surprising.

Alternatively, another powerful figure that might have effected such a dramatic transformation of the town centre would be a king (*tyrannus* is Gildas' expression) who may either have risen out of the remnants of the town's aristocracy who survived the *c.*540 catastrophe, or even perhaps by other ambitious people from outside, filling a perceived vacuum following the death of the old society at Wroxeter. For example, the nascent kingdom of Powys to the west. Conceivably, the person responsible could even have been the bishop in a minor king's court, brought in by the king to protect his new flock. Whoever the authority was, he not only turned the site of a great public building into a private demesne but also, apparently, ordered the extension of the reconstruction into the surrounding *insulae*.

Certainly, the appropriation of public space in this way does demonstrate far-reaching changes in attitudes. The introverted arrangement of the revamped basilica site suggests that people wanted to live more privately. This is reflected too in the abandonment of the large open-air market area offered by the former basilica. Indeed, as first arranged, there was no provision in the new scheme for markets, the stalls on the gravel street only appearing gradually and probably unofficially, in the manner of a Middle Eastern *souk*. Such changes might well be interpreted as a fear of having large numbers of people meeting together and if so then the rebuilding and reorganisation may reflect the consequences of the 536-40 Event and its aftermath, the *mortalitas magna* ('Great Death') that reached Britain in the mid-sixth century. This disastrous epidemic, almost certainly bubonic plague, is first reported in the east in 542 but quickly spread westwards reaching Britain by 547 at least when Maelgwn, King of Gwynedd, was killed by it. It may have reached Wroxeter too and decimated the population there. The effects of plague on the town may well have been dramatic but not necessarily catastrophic, as is demonstrated by the apparently minimal long-term effects of the Black Death of the fourteenth century and London's survival of the plague of 1665-6. When plague arrived, those who could fled, perhaps to a site like Whitley, whilst those who could not stayed on. The disease will certainly have been felt most keenly among the weakest in society – the young, sick and elderly – but may have left the bulk of the population unscathed. Emotionally, however, the effects will have been enormous so it is perhaps not surprising that, if the *mortalitas magna* did affect Wroxeter, the survivors will have been more wary of associating freely with their fellow citizens.

Although the buildings on the baths basilica and its immediate surroundings can be interpreted as being associated with Building 10, the rebuilding was not limited to that area. On the street frontage north of Building 10, that is on the other side of the gravel street, the old buildings were swept away and replaced by at least six buildings, with space for a seventh (Buildings 45–51) put up on plots of varying widths which conformed once again to Roman measurements (**64**). The most common width was 6m (20 Roman feet) whilst others were slightly larger at 7m (24 Roman feet). These houses were later replaced by fewer and more substantial buildings (7, 9, 13, 15 and 22), nearly all of which must have been two-storied (see **63, colour plate 21**). Like their predecessors they too conformed to Roman measurements. All of these, as with Building 10, were built in the Roman fashion with grand porches and steps and often to Roman dimensions. Many were timber-framed but others had clay walls or were of mixed construction. The differing construction methods argues strongly that although the plots may have been of standard widths, the buildings themselves were built by individual families, as is also hinted at by evidence for the use of salvaged timbers in some places. Between Building 10 and the street frontage to the north the gravel street seems to have been gradually colonised by a number of lightweight structures, Buildings 12, 40–44, which were too small to have been houses but could have been stalls or shops, presumably the latest in the long tradition of such structures which had previously been located within the porticoes and then inside the basilica's shell. In support of this interpretation, a small open-fronted structure, Building 26, which was situated on the cobble street remnant between the Watling Street and the gravel street, may be seen as a booth controlling pedestrians in and out of the street market.

On the west portico a sequence of buildings of more substantial design was found. These were erected in pairs over three successive phases (Buildings 38 and 39, 33 and 34, 25 and 29), one of each pair being deliberately placed so as to block the main entrance into the former basilica as though controlling access to the space beyond (**65**). Building 34 in the middle phase had a substantial outdoor hearth by it, in and around which was found burnt wheat implying that in this phase at least these buildings were houses rather than shops. Further structures, Buildings 37 and 32, were also traced south of these buildings. Similar buildings were observed in the excavations on the por-

63 *A possible reconstruction by Peter Scholefield and Heather Bird of the evidence seen in* **62**. *The size of these buildings might seem too great but are certainly possible given comparable medieval buildings. The use of timber framing meant that buildings could be large without using deep foundations*

tico outside the *macellum*, which itself is likely still to have been in use. The *macellum*'s sturdy construction and small rooms would have made it easy to maintain and the date of its final decay and ruin is by no means clear.

In all, the excavations on the baths basilica site produced a startling total of 33 buildings in this period, hardly evidence for the decline of the community. Furthermore, it is possible to demonstrate that this spate of new buildings was not confined to the site of the baths (**66**). Earlier excavations in other *insulae* in the city centre too found similar structures but did not understand them fully. On *insula* 9 south of the baths Dame Kathleen Kenyon had found a position for a horizontal timber supporting a wall on the site of the town house she excavated; one of the present authors found evidence for timber buildings on *insulae* 2 and 6 to the north, north-east and east of the baths; and Donald Atkinson had noted structures in the forum courtyard in *insula* 4 which, although he did not interpret them as houses, resembled stables he had seen behind the lines on the Western Front in the First World War. He also found a large bread oven on the forum portico which may be the same date as that found on the west portico of the baths basilica. Certainly, it was abundantly clear from the excavations on the baths basilica site that only the most meticulous excavation would understand the slight traces left by these buildings so it is not surprising that earlier excavators had not understood fully what they had uncovered.

The full extent of occupation at this time is not yet clear but it can be suggested that the northern part of the city, including the Bell Brook valley, was abandoned since Kathleen

64 *The remains of Building 47 (located beneath Building 9 on **62**). The wall lines show as a line of cobble and rubble curving round gently to form a right angle (P). This curving corner suggests a clay-walled structure, perhaps within internal timber reinforcement. The mirror image of the wall lies in the foreground. The break between the two walls represents the doorway. The width of the building conforms to 20 Roman feet (6m)*

Kenyon found evidence for a refurbishment of the first-century ditch on the south side of the valley. She dated this refurbishment to the fourth century but at that time the full circuit of the city defences was still in use, as is shown by its own remodelling. It seems more probable that the abandonment of the northern part of the city fits in with the troubled times of the fifth and sixth centuries. The rest of the defensive circuit, however, is likely to have remained in use, albeit perhaps in a dilapidated condition.

Intriguingly, there is now evidence that buildings such as those just described were being built in the countryside too. At Whitley Grange, the mosaic room and the south-west and south-east corners of the courtyard were redeveloped as the sites of lightweight buildings which in places clearly obscured the walls of the previous villa and, in the case of the mosaic room, actually cut into the floor (see **57**). One of the buildings had a rubble platform beneath a mortar and clay floor similar to those seen at Wroxeter. Dating evidence for these buildings was sparse but included very late Roman pottery. A remanent magnetic date for the last firing of the bath house of 420–520 was also of significance since material from the baths appeared to have been used to build the rubble platform in the south-west corner.

Despite such extensive occupation at Wroxeter we should ask whether this still constituted town life. Clearly this is a question that might not have concerned the people at

65 *A photograph showing a diagonal path leading into the shell of the basilica from the west portico. The path is defined by worn stones which contrast sharply with the unworn rubble areas behind, the two areas being divided by a fence. The north threshold of the former basilica lies in the foreground*

the time: they may well have considered themselves to be living within a town even though it had none of the recognised institutions, public buildings, and grand houses of an early Roman town. Nonetheless, a number of features can be highlighted about these buildings. First, their construction was carefully planned and executed using a large work force to dig out the street and demolish parts of the basilica in a controlled way. Furthermore, the new buildings were skilfully constructed to Roman measurements using a trained labour force. Their presence strongly suggests that there was still scope for specialised trades within the population, as does the encroachment of a market onto the gravel street. Goods other than those locally produced must have been rare indeed: only one possible import was identified, an oil or wine jar from Palestine whose contents were perhaps destined for church rather than a table. This exotic piece may have been brought to Wroxeter either by the southern trade route, along the Severn or perhaps via Cirencester or Bath since both have produced similar wares. An alternative route is that from the north via Meols or Chester, since the area of the Wirral has produced sixth-century Byzantine coins and a small pilgrim flask of similar date from the monastery of St Menas in Egypt. The links between what is happening at Wroxeter and at other erstwhile Roman towns in the west of Britain is not limited to trade. Excavations within the precinct of the temple of Sulis Minerva at Bath and its associated baths produced evidence for prolonged use of the floors there which were repaired

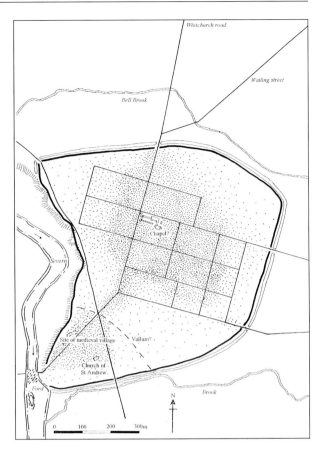

66 *A plan of the sub-Roman town, c.500–650. The shaded areas in the town centre and at the ford are the known extent of occupation but may have been linked together by further buildings, as suggested here*

and maintained probably well into the fifth or even sixth century before they were inundated by the spring waters. At Chester, excavations at Hunter Street within a large courtyard found building platforms very similar to those found at Wroxeter although the small area available for excavation meant that they could not be fully understood. Indeed, Chester too may have had a bishop since a recently discovered lead salt pan found at Shavington appears to refer to an *episcopus* named Viventius, a common name used by the early Christians, as exemplified by a priest of that name commemorated on a Scottish tombstone dated to about 500. Unfortunately, not enough is known about the Christian community at this time to determine whether Viventius was a bishop (at this early date the title *episcopus* could be used to mean overseer) nor, if he was, whether he served at Chester or Wroxeter.

The picture that emerges, therefore, is that not just Wroxeter but other towns in the west also survived into the post-Roman period, even if not in a form that might be termed 'classical'. Although this society was initially thoroughly Romanized, it increasingly became more and more isolated and introverted with each town concentrating on holding its own territory, usually through the authority of the church manifest either in the form of the town's bishop or, increasingly, by the monastic communities which were springing up in Britain from the mid-sixth century. Quite how these communities were accommodated within the existing ecclesiastical hierarchy is unclear but at least one important monastery is known in Cornovian territory, that at Bangor-is-y-Coed, about halfway between Chester and Wroxeter. Their monks were involved in the Battle of Chester in 613 when they were massacred almost to a man by the Northumbrians.

The decline of Roman structures of government throughout the fifth century soon allowed the tribal aristocracy to re-establish more traditional Celtic forms of government under chiefs and kings to fill the power vacuum. Naturally, these new kingdoms first seem to have arisen in those areas where Romanization had had least impact, as in the heartland of Wales where by the sixth century the old tribal groups had been transformed into kingdoms. These kingdoms and their rulers were listed by Gildas, who may have lived at Bangor-is-y-Coed and whose work *De Excidio Britonum* ('On the Ruin of Britain') was written in the first half of the sixth century. He talks of a period of peace which may be about to end because of the wickedness and sinfulness of these rulers whom he castigates in turn. The work is valuable not least for the confirmation of the names of the kingdoms, even though their rulers are not generally identified directly, but also because it provides a useful insight into the society of that period. Clearly Gildas was expecting his work to be read by an educated, Latin-reading, public which consisted not only of his fellow clergy but of secular people too, perhaps those attending court. Gildas argues that the Romans had left Britain because the country was ungrateful and undeserving of help, not least due to the many usurpers that had appeared at the end of the Roman period. The appearance of the Anglo-Saxons was God's punishment on the British, cleansing the towns and their people by destroying them. His dire warning, and the ultimate purpose of the book, is that the process will happen again unless the British clergy and kings mend their ways.

For the rulers of the new kingdoms of the west, Gildas can only have been a minor irritant and there were more pressing concerns that they will have been dealing with. Inevitably, these men will have attempted to legitimise their rule by claiming that they were directly descended from the late Roman state. This may have been satisfactory in the countryside where tribal values had never been deeply submerged or altered by Romanization, but authoritarian rulers (Gildas' *tyranni*) may have been less appealing in the towns where the inhabitants were used to a degree of self-rule. Rulers could have overcome this problem by the simple expedient of living in the town, but towns were not attractive to secular rulers and in any case they were unlikely to have worried about the opinions of the citizens. Rather, the documentary and archaeological evidence show unequivocally that kings chose to live like their ancestors in prehistoric times in heavily defended hillforts such as Dinorben or Dinas Emrys, both seats of one of the most powerful of the new kingdoms, Gwynedd, which occupied all of north-west Wales. To its east, roughly the former territory of the *Ordovices* and *Deceangli*, lay the heartland of the kingdom of Powys but, as we shall see, there is evidence in the shadowy traditions of the Welsh epic poetry that Powys originally extended eastwards to include much of Cornovian territory. The same sources also hint that their kingdom was a loose confederation of minor rulers or leaders under the overlordship of the King of Powys. If so, it is likely that Wroxeter and Chester were within this confederation whilst still retaining their status as quasi-autonomous units along with their immediate territory. Quite how such an arrangement came about is wholly unclear but ultimately rested on force. The King of Powys must have been able to call upon a levy of fighting troops which the towns are unlikely to have been able

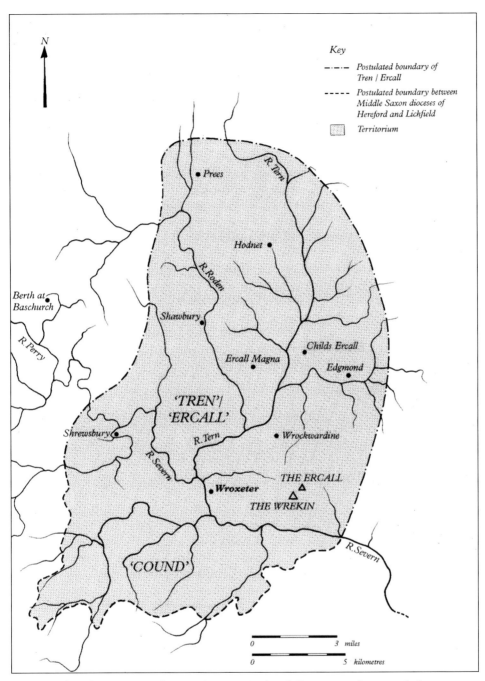

67 *A hypothetical reconstruction of Wroxeter's territory in the sub-Roman, or perhaps even the late Roman, period*

to match. The towns will have felt increasingly vulnerable given the renewed Anglo-Saxon expansion and may have decided eventually to sacrifice their independence in favour of the protection of a powerful overlord. In return, the King will have defended these large concentrations of population from attack. The price of such an alliance could have been met from a proportion of the town's tax revenues, by now probably paid exclusively in kind. If so, we can envisage the king and his court visiting Wroxeter on a regular basis to collect their dues and to assert their dominance over the town's rulers and population.

Despite the difficulties of using Dark Age texts to reconstruct history, the Welsh poems preserved as the *Englynion* have two particularly important texts concerning the early kingdom of Powys and its relationship to the other Welsh and Anglo-Saxon kingdoms. These are *Marwnnd Cynddylan* ('The Lament for Cynddylan') and *Canu Heledd* ('The Song of Heledd'). The first tells of the death in battle of Cynddylan, the king of Powys whose family were the Cyndrwyn. There are hints in the poem that the king was over-lord over several other princes, including the House of the Cadelling. The *Canu Heledd* is a lament not just for Cynddylan, Heledd's brother, but the loss of the whole kingdom which, the place names in the poem make clear, included much of the area around Wroxeter. The poems place Cynddylan's hall at *Pengwern* but unfortunately the site is unknown although various suggestions have been made. Of these, the least likely is Shrewsbury which does not seem to have been occupied before the eighth century. Other suggestions include the Berth at Baschurch (**colour plate 22**), favoured because the poem states that Cynddylan was buried at the *Churches of Bassa*, or the Breiddin where an important Dark Age enclosure, New Pieces, is known, or even possibly the hillfort at Nesscliffe. Both of these latter places are visible from Wroxeter.

From the mid-sixth century, the Anglo-Saxon kingdoms had begun to grow again, as Gildas had warned they would, and were pushing westwards and northwards. In 577 at the battle of Dyrham in Gloucestershire the 'kings' of Cirencester, Gloucester and Bath were defeated and presumably their towns fell to the Anglo-Saxons. By the early seventh century, the Northumbrians under King Æthelfrith had crossed the Pennines and exerted control over the former British kingdoms in Elmet, Cumbria and Lancashire, and had then crossed the Mersey to attack the former territory of the *Cornovii*. Their attack culminated in the battle of Chester in about 613. This ushered in a long sequence of wars involving an alliance between the Welsh kingdoms of Gwynedd and Powys under Cadwallon and Cynddylan respectively with the Anglo-Saxon kingdom of Mercia under their pagan king Penda. The war was conducted throughout the north-western midlands with known battles being fought at *Meigen*, a site somewhere in Powys in about 630, and at *Maeserfelth/Cogwy* in 642. The site of this battle is often identified as Oswestry and if so this too was in Powys. Here a humbling defeat was inflicted on the Northumbrians, led by King Oswald who lost his life. After this victory, the Anglo-Saxon and British alliance went on the offensive, invading Northumbrian territory but were themselves beaten at the River *Winwæd*, near Leeds in 655, a battle in which Penda, certainly, and Cynddylan, probably, lost their lives. After this, the Northumbrians kept Mercia under its control until Penda's son, Wulfhere, was able to exert independence after 657. From that date until his death in 674, also in battle against the Northumbrians, Wulfhere strengthened the Mercian kingdom by attacking to the east and south, his alliance with the kingdoms of Powys and Gwynedd protecting his west flank. Mercia once again fell under Northumbrian influence from 674 until the Northumbrian kingdom was catastrophically defeated at *Nechtansmere* in Pictland in 685 after which its aggressive power was permanently ended.

The long sequence of battles preserved in the poems and historical sources is by no means complete but fully demonstrates the stormy nature of the alliance between the Welsh kingdoms of Gwynedd and Powys and the Anglo-Saxons of Mercia in the face of the aggressive expansion of Northumbria. The alliance was of considerable value to the Mercians since it not only enabled them to fight Northumbria but, more importantly, meant that they could attack to the south and east of their kingdom knowing that they would not be under threat from the west. For the Welsh kingdoms the alliance brought security in two ways: it prevented the Mercians from attacking them and protected them from the aggression of the Northumbrians. But despite this, the alliance cannot have been an easy one. There must have been a degree of suspicion from all sides, not least because up to his death Penda remained a pagan whereas the Welsh kings were Christian. Furthermore, there must have been a price to pay for a military alliance with such a powerful kingdom, and it will almost certainly have been paid by the weakest member of the alliance, Powys. Gwynedd, remote in its mountain vastness of Snowdonia, was not vulnerable to Mercia but could be attacked by sea by Northumbria. It will have been able to negotiate the treaty from a position of relative strength given its resources in manpower and food. Powys, however, had felt the full force of the Northumbrians in the attack on Chester and at *Meigen* and can only have survived these defeats in a weakened state. We cannot know what price Powys had to pay but an obvious resource that the kingdom could call upon was land which the kingdom did not deem to be especially valuable or which might be expendable politically. Since the centre of Powys' power was in the foothills of the Welsh mountains, on the western border of Shropshire and Cheshire, it seems likely that the land they ceded to Mercia was all that which lay on the east bank of the Severn, which included Wroxeter and the greater part of its probable territory. An echo of this is found in the *Canu Heledd* which, however, casts the transition in a much more lurid light, lamenting the defeat of Cynddylan by the Anglo-Saxons and the loss of 'the fair town between the Tren and Trafal'. The gaunt beauty of the poem, with its aching refrain on the loss of loved ones and of past happiness, has blinded many to the realities of seventh-century *Realpolitik*. The real context of this poem lies not in the seventh century where it is set, but in the ninth century when it was written. By then, the alliance with Mercia had long been ended and the Anglo-Saxons instead of stopping at the Severn had vastly expanded their territory to swamp much of western Powys, giving permanent form to their border with the huge ditch and bank which bears the name of the most famous of Mercia's kings, Offa. The kingdom of Powys increasingly found itself squeezed between the ever-aggressive Mercia and their equally unrelenting Welsh neighbours in Gwynedd. It was hardly surprising that some 200 years later they should remember their days of glory in the seventh century with a mixture of pride and sorrow.

There is some echo also among the Mercians of these lands that they acquired. In the late seventh- or early eighth-century text, the *Tribal Hidage*, a document relating to the calculation of tax and war services due to the Mercian king, various peoples are listed as being peripheral to the core of the kingdom which was centred on Staffordshire. Among these are mentioned the *Wrocensætna*, a term which can mean either 'people of the

Wrekin' or 'people of Wroxeter'. If the latter, then this suggests that Wroxeter still had a vestigial importance and this may be confirmed by a curious anomaly in the medieval diocesan boundary between Lichfield and Hereford noted and discussed by Dr Steven Bassett (**67**). Quite when this boundary was set up is not known but Lichfield Diocese was founded as a see in the late seventh century by St Chad and rapidly established itself as the dominant church in Mercia. The boundary of its diocese with its ecclesiastical neighbour, Hereford, is drawn along the line of the River Severn except for a large area of land opposite Wroxeter. This, the parish of Cound, lies in Lichfield and its position may well echo the boundary of Wroxeter's civilian *territorium*. The northern part of the territory, on the east bank of the Severn, is probably that area referred to in the *Canu Heledd* as *Tren* which, through a simple linguistic reversal wrought by the English, has become the modern River Tern, an important tributary of the Severn which joins it by Wroxeter. The Anglo-Saxon name for this same territory appears to have been Ercall, a name perhaps derived from the small hill to the north of the Wrekin still called the Ercall (the name means 'gravel hill'). Two other Ercall names are also known in the river valley of the Tern, Childs Ercall and High Ercall (Ercall Magna), and the association between Ercall and *Tren* thus seems highly plausible. From these snippets of evidence, therefore, it is possible to suggest that the territory of Wroxeter consisted of the river basin of the Tern, a broad expanse of land with Shrewsbury at its western edge, and a block of land drained by the Cound Brook.

We cannot hope to prove what actually happened but if this reconstruction resembles the truth then Wroxeter's fate as a town will have been sealed, since King Penda will not have wanted a town, or given his religious beliefs, its bishop on his doorstep. Furthermore he will not have wanted Wroxeter as a capital since he had capitals, first at Tamworth and later at Lichfield. Wroxeter, no longer part of Powys and suddenly situated rather precariously on the border of two kingdoms which were soon to become hostile, could not hope to survive. Its people seem largely to have dispersed, perhaps moving west to mix with their kin in Powys or east to find favour with the Mercians who certainly included a substantial number of British people within their kingdom. The town dwindled away to become a mere village at a crossing point of the Severn.

The archaeological evidence on the baths basilica site fits in with this scenario. It shows that the community lasted there for probably at least 75 years after the major re-organisation since in places buildings were renewed three times over, until eventually the occupation ceased. There was no evidence in the archaeological record for a dramatic end to the town. Rather the buildings seem to have been dismantled, although Building 31 was left to collapse, presumably because being of stone its constituent parts were not capable of recycling. There was one last building, Building 4, erected partly overlying the site of Building 10, and, more tellingly, a burial was cut through the platform of Building 11 (**colour plate 23**). A radiocarbon date for this burial showed that this man must have been buried between 600–790, and this must have taken place on a deserted site. Another burial is also known on the street outside the forum portico. They surely attest to the desertion of the former town centre in favour of the site of the present-day village.

8 Saxon, medieval and later Wroxeter

The demise of Wroxeter as a town did not spell the end of settlement there. The site was still habitable and since people needed to use the Roman road system and with it the ford across the Severn there will have been some who stayed on within the city walls. All the evidence seems to point to a shift in the remaining population to the southern end of the city, where the present village is located. The density of Roman settlement in this area is uncertain since it is masked by the modern village but at least one late city house is known from its fine mosaic found in 1827 (**colour plate 15**) and the remains of other houses have been discovered elsewhere in the village. There may have been a number of factors which led to this area being chosen for the small-scale settlement which developed there (**68**). Most important of these was the Watling Street river crossing. The new location was defined to the south by a small unnamed brook which had been used as one of the city ditches when the defences were first laid out in the second century. North of this brook were the city defences themselves consisting here of two broad banks separated by a ditch. These defences extended down and along the river cliff on the western side and curved round on the eastern side to encompass both the village and land which became the village's fields in the medieval period, where ridge-and-furrow can still be seen. To the north there are the remains of a slight bank and ditch which cut across the south-west corner of the defended area enclosing most of the known village. The area thus created was not heavily fortified but promised some security for its inhabitants.

The date of this newly-defended area is unknown and will only be discovered by further excavation. If we are right in thinking that occupation continued here unbroken from the time when the city was still in existence then the defensive bank cutting off the settlement from the city will only have become necessary on the latter's abandonment, perhaps in the mid-seventh century. The inhabitants of the settlement, like those of the city before them, are likely to have been British and thus predominantly Christian. It is possible that even at this early date an Anglo-Saxon overlord may have settled here, perhaps on the site of the medieval manor house in the south-west corner of the village. We can safely assume, however, that there was a priest to minister to the community and the surrounding countryside although at this early date, in the seventh and early eighth century, the Mercian kingdom is unlikely to have had a parochial organisation. In Celtic areas of Britain, where Roman life had never been firmly established or had never been established at all, it was quite usual for a small monastic community to take on this role.

This being so, it is possible that Wroxeter's church had a monastic foundation. Some support for this can be gathered from the known history and archaeology of the church but it can also be supported from the topographical position of the village. As already outlined, it is clearly defined by ditches or by natural features such as watercourses, themselves emphasised by ditches and banks. Such boundaries are an essential feature of early monasteries since they represent the division between what is secular and what is profane. Celtic monasteries, built in remote places and often on previously unoccupied sites, defined their precincts by a bank and ditch (known as a *vallum*), as at Iona, or let nature define it for them as on the island monasteries of Skellig Michael and Lindisfarne. Monasteries in early Christian England, often founded from the seventh and eighth centuries by Celtic monks, were more constrained in their choice of sites. Isolation might be found by locating the monastery within an old Roman fort, as at Portchester or Bradwell, where the thick walls of these Saxon Shore forts kept worldly concerns away from the community inside, or on hilltops. Later, Saxon monasteries, which were increasingly located within towns for safety, usually defined their precincts by building a wall. Wroxeter with its reused city defences and slight earthworks fits well with the pattern that would be expected of a Celtic monastic site defined by a *vallum*. Other evidence can also be produced to argue the case that Wroxeter's church was in origin a British monastery. For example, the present church of St Andrew does not have a true east–west alignment as is usual for a church but lies at 23° east of north, on the same alignment in fact as the Roman street grid. Significantly, the church also sits on a major junction between two of the city's former roads – the Watling Street which ran in front of the church but some distance forward of it, and another east-west road running down to the ford. Thus the church was not only built while the roads were still in use but also in the most prominent position within the new settlement.

Within the fabric of the Church of St Andrew at Wroxeter one can still see evidence of its antiquity (**69**). In the central part of its north wall, large stones looted from Roman public buildings have been reused to build a simple structure typical of the earliest type of Anglo-Saxon architecture. A number of architectural features can be used to date this wall, such as its small round-headed window (now blocked) and the use of a building technique characteristic of Anglo-Saxon masonry – side-alternate quoining – so called because the corner displays alternately a narrow or broad face of stone. The full plan of this church is not known since later modifications have removed all the other walls but the position of the Saxon south wall (now rebuilt on a different alignment) is known and there was almost certainly a square chancel at the east end. There could conceivably have been a tower at the west end as was common on the larger and more important churches of the period, and if so the foundations of it might yet be seen in excavation within the church, but equally a very simple design, like that at Bishop Escomb, Co. Durham could fit the known evidence.

The precise date of the north wall of the present church is uncertain: its simple plan may put it into the earliest phase of stone-built Anglo-Saxon churches of the eighth century but its projecting string course at the top of the wall is not closely dateable. A late ninth-century date for the church may be suggested on the basis of a strap-tag found in the fill of a robbing trench dug through the baths basilica which suggests that the Anglo-Saxons were robbing stone from the former city centre at that time, but there is no positive link between this find and the church of St Andrew (**colour plate 24**). Even

68 *An aerial view of Wroxeter village – the church is conspicuous. The River Severn lies to the left with the ford below the island, the latter a feature created in the Middle Ages by digging a channel to create locations for fish weirs. The compact nature of the village is evident, as is its relationship to the centre of the Roman city which lies at the top of the photograph*

69 *A measured drawing of the north side of St Andrew's church, Wroxeter. The large stones of the Anglo-Saxon wall are prominent in the centre. The Norman chancel is to the left*

if the church does prove to be later, rather than earlier, Anglo-Saxon, we do not know whether this was the first building on the site. Certainly there are hints that there may have been an earlier church here. The most important pieces of evidence are the shaft of a cross flanked by two carved stone panels showing animals, which have been built into the south wall of the church since the 1760s. Another carved stone piece of similar date and style, showing snakes being pecked by ducks, now rests at the foot of the present chancel arch (**colour plate 25**). An engraving of mid-eighteenth century date shows that until then these pieces had together formed part of a cross standing in the churchyard (**70**). The date of this monument can be fixed quite closely to the time of King Offa (d. 796) by parallels with an important group of carvings of similar style found elsewhere in the country, most notably at the important Anglo-Saxon monastery at Breedon-on-the-Hill, Leicestershire. This group, known as the Mercian School of sculpture, shows close affinities with art of the Carolingian court which in its turn draws closely on late Roman art. Presumably, this cross was associated either with the present church, in which case it would date that building, or was associated with an earlier timber church or even stood alone as a preaching cross. Its late eighth- or early ninth-century date certainly shows that an Anglo-Saxon Christian community was in existence by that date and since it is thought that urban life ceased at Wroxeter in the mid-seventh century, this leaves only just over a century to bridge between the proposed British community and the known Anglo-Saxon Christian one. Some pottery of a post-Roman, but not Anglo-Saxon, style found during repair work on the church does appear to confirm that the site was occupied during this period but the material remains of a church or other building of this date would be difficult to recognise archaeologically as it would also have been in timber and the traces of this may well have been removed by

70 *An eighteenth-century drawing of Wroxeter cross. The upper part of the north side is still visible in the south wall of the church (see colour plate 25)*

later church building or by grave-digging. It may yet be discovered accidentally, but for the present we have to turn to the historical sources to find evidence of an earlier Christian community on the site.

Two pieces of historical evidence can be used to demonstrate the importance of Wroxeter's church in this early period. The first is the entry in *Domesday Book* for Wroxeter and the second is the reconstruction by Dr Steven Bassett of the boundary of the early parishes in and around Wroxeter itself discussed in the previous chapter. The *Domesday Book* entry for Wroxeter states that the church there had four priests. This indicates a very large parish, quite out of keeping with the small community recorded in the village in the same survey, and suggests that Wroxeter had an anomalous status in the pre-Anglo-Saxon period possibly based on its suggested foundation as a British monastery. This status ensured that Wroxeter continued to be a place of some importance in the eighth to eleventh centuries.

The Anglo-Saxon settlement in Wroxeter, epitomised both by the free-standing cross and its church, was certainly not a monastic community. Instead, it appears to have become a village with a manor house. Our first solid historical knowledge of the village people comes from *Domesday Book* which records that it contained seven villagers and four smallholders in addition to the four priests. These figures of course only account for the heads of households and not for their families and dependants. In addition to the villagers, the land held by the Lord of the Manor was farmed by seven slaves of both sexes. At the time of the conquest, the Lord of the Manor was Thored but under the Normans the land was held by the Reginald, Sheriff under Earl Roger de Montgomery. After Roger's death, it passed to the Fitz Alan family who held it until the Earls of Arundel acquired the manor in the early fourteenth century.

Our picture of life within and around Wroxeter before the Norman conquest is only fitfully illuminated by archaeology. In addition to the evidence from the church, there is a collection of metal-detected finds of late Saxon date from Norton, the small hamlet immediately outside Wroxeter's north gate. These objects include two strap tags of ninth- and tenth-century date, while a stirrup mount of tenth-century date is known from the village of Withington 2 miles (3km) north of Wroxeter. Upton Magna, the village lying 2 miles (3km) north-west of Wroxeter has a church with masonry derived from the public buildings of Roman Wroxeter, as do the Churches of St Eata at Atcham and that of St Mary and St Andrew at Condover whilst the fonts at Wroxeter and at Berrington have been carved from Roman column bases (**71**). Another church, that of St Samson's, Cressage, although now destroyed, is also of interest in that it had a dedication to a Celtic saint, and the place name itself ('Christ's Oak') refers to an early Christian community there. In legend, it was a meeting place between St Augustine and the British bishops. All of these churches lie within the putative territory controlled by Wroxeter at the time of the Anglo-Saxon conquest and suggests that they too may have an early Christian origin, and additionally may later have had a right to use the valuable building stone that the former city could provide. Such pieces of evidence show that the modern villages of the area have their roots deep into the Anglo-Saxon period and it may be that there was some continuity of settlement between the Roman and early medieval periods. For example, the farms at Uckington and at Chilton Farm, Atcham, north-east and due west of Wroxeter respectively, both show evidence for occupation in the Roman and medieval periods and it is perhaps more likely than not that settlement may be assumed for the intervening period, despite the lack of artefacts to prove it. On the other hand there are farms, like that at Norton, which have no Roman or prehistoric precursor and suggest a new foundation.

One site known from this shadowy time between the Romano-British collapse and the Norman conquest is that found at Frog Hall, Atcham 3 miles (4km) north-west of Wroxeter (**72**). Here aerial photographs have detected a set of buildings whose plans are very similar to timber halls excavated at the seventh-century royal site at Yeavering, Northumberland and, nearer, from Hatton Rock, Warwickshire. Yeavering is known to be the palace of *Ad Gefrin* referred to in Bede's *Ecclesiastical History* and this has led to the suggestion that the buildings at Frog Hall too should be seen as a regal site of the same date. This is perhaps pushing the evidence too far since we have no date for the buildings except from their style and more importantly there is no documentary evidence for Anglo-Saxon kings in Shropshire. Nonetheless, Frog Hall appears to be a prestigious early Anglo-Saxon site and is the sort of settlement that a powerful *thegn* might live in. There may be a similar hall yet to be found at Wroxeter, although none is known from aerial photography or geophysics, and the impression generated by the Frog Hall settlement is that it stands in deliberate isolation from the pattern of known Roman sites, not least Wroxeter itself. If so, it may be seen as an intermediary settlement between the Roman city and Shrewsbury.

71 *The Romanesque fonts of Wroxeter and Berrington churches. Wroxeter's font was carved from a very large column base, upended and hollowed out. Berrington's font was carved from a smaller base, which has been elaborately decorated with seven heads, a cockerel, a candlestick and a ?dog*

143

The basic stability of the landscape pattern suggested by the limited archaeological evidence may be contrasted by place name evidence. Studies have shown that nearly all the place names of Shropshire have an Anglo-Saxon origin with few obvious references to the Celtic or Roman names that the settlements must have had in the Roman period, although the river names and those of other major landscape features tend to be Celtic in origin. This might suggest that the Anglo-Saxons moved into an abandoned landscape and thus had to invent new place names but the archaeological evidence does not bear this out since there is no archaeobotanical sign of woodland regeneration that would normally occur if the land had been abandoned. Instead, new Anglo-Saxon settlements seem to be occurring in the anciently wooded areas of the landscape generating a flush of -ley place names, as in Madeley, Dawley, etc. which refer to a clearing in a wood (OE -*leah*). In other words, the new settlers are being forced onto the marginal land since the best land is already occupied by the existing population. How then did the place names change from Celtic to Anglo-Saxon? What may be suggested is that the existing British population rapidly adopted Anglo-Saxon as their first language, as happened throughout England at this time, and that Celtic and Latin swiftly died out as living languages. The process would have been encouraged by the fact that the new ruling élite was Anglo-Saxon and the administration of the area would have been carried out in Old English. Young men and women who wished to take part in the new society would have had to adapt to the new language much in the way that their forebears had adopted Latin when the Romans arrived.

Thus one can envisage the initial Anglo-Saxon settlement in the seventh and eighth centuries as being a largely peaceful and perhaps even prosperous time. Certainly, under King Offa, the Mercian kingdom enjoyed a period of supremacy which was only ended by the Viking raids and settlement at the very end of the eighth century. The impact of the Vikings on the area was marginal but did affect Shropshire in the later ninth century with raids penetrating to Bridgnorth in the south-east of the county and to Buttington in the west. The latter location was the site of a battle which turned the Vikings back and prevented the area falling into their hands, and by the early tenth century the Kings of Wessex under Alfred, his family, and descendants gradually pushed the Vikings back to the north and east, away from Shropshire and the west country. From the early tenth century both Shropshire and Cheshire were under the control of Ethelred and his redoubtable wife Æthelflæd, sister of Alfred the Great, who implemented Alfred's policy of consolidation and protection of the newly-created shires through the foundation and encouragement of fortified places, or *burhs* as they were called in Old English. These were strongly defensible sites which were in effect towns whose inhabitants had a duty to act as a militia to defend themselves rather than relying on the king's army to assist them. If Viking raids took place, the rural population could flee to the town with their possessions and there seek shelter and protection. These *burhs* were founded along the frontier with the Viking-controlled land, the Danelaw, and are known to have existed at Bridgnorth (founded 912) and Shrewsbury ('the fortified place in the scrub') with further sites in Cheshire at Eddisbury (914), Chester (907), Runcorn (915) and Thelwall (919) and in Staffordshire at Stafford (913) and Tamworth (913).

The foundation of Shrewsbury, certainly by 901 but probably at least 50–100 years before, was the final death knell to any thought of re-founding Wroxeter. The new site lay on the edge of Wroxeter's territory, as reconstructed by Dr Steven Bassett, and had a

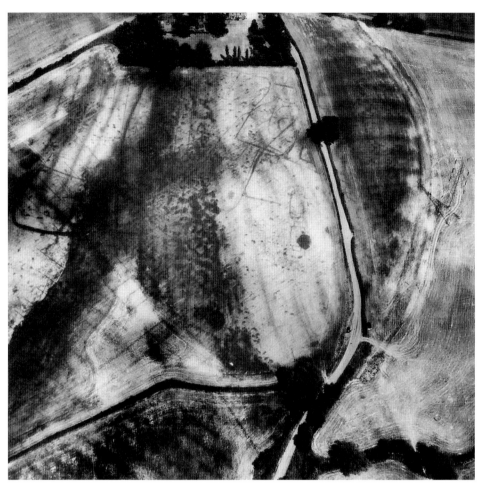

72 *An aerial photograph of the possible Anglo-Saxon halls at Frog Hall, Atcham. The halls lie in the centre of the picture, partly destroyed by a circular black feature (probably a later quarry pit)*

number of advantages over its Roman predecessor. Most important of these was that Shrewsbury was a much more defensible site than the old Roman city since it was surrounded on three sides by the River Severn with only one approach by land, later to be defended by the Norman castle. The strong defensive position afforded by Shrewsbury's natural topography made the site an ideal location for a *burh* with the minimum of effort and earth-movement. Once founded, Shrewsbury flourished as the capital of the newly-founded county of Shropshire and any residual influence that Wroxeter had retained rapidly ebbed away.

Despite this, there is evidence that Wroxeter continued to grow in size as a village. In about 1190, the chancel of the church was rebuilt after it had been donated to Haughmond Abbey by Richard Fitz Alan in 1155, a grant confirmed by papal decree in 1172. The masonry used is still clearly derived from the Roman city since some of the blocks of stone show evidence of Lewis slots and the money saved on quarrying fresh stone was instead expended on the fine dog-tooth carving of the string course running below the six round-headed windows, three each on the north and south sides and the five-light east window, and on the elaborate Romanesque-style priest's doorway which is still partly visible on the south side. In places, the plaster rendering of the church survives showing that in common with the Norman fashion, the exterior of the church had been whitewashed and lined with false-jointing. The doubling of the internal area of the church that this rebuilding represents surely argues for a steadily growing population. Although Wroxeter was not the primary residence of the Fitz Alans, at least one member, John Fitz Alan, is recorded as dying there. His widow, Matilda, continued to live in the village with her second husband, Richard de Amundevill, until her death in 1283 when it was recorded that the mill at Wroxeter and its associated fish ponds were valued at £12 9s 2d *per annum*.

The location of the manor house was identified by Thomas Wright in the 1860s as lying about 50m south-west of the church and a recent survey has identified both the platform for this manor house, its associated fish ponds and the site of the mill (**73**). The ponds were created by digging into the back of the city ramparts and diverting into them the small unnamed stream which ran in the outer city ditch, the overflow going into the Severn south of the ford. How long the Manor continued in occupation is unclear but it may have fallen into disuse when it came into the possession of the Earls of Arundel in the early fourteenth century.

The structural evidence of the church points to a steady growth in the community at Wroxeter so that by the time of the next documentary source, a rental of 1350, the population had grown from the seven free households of the late eleventh century to 33 families. The increasing size and wealth of this community was expressed most obviously in the construction of a new south aisle to the church in the late thirteenth or early fourteenth century. This involved taking down the south wall of the Saxon church, replacing it with an arcade, and locating the new wall about 3m further south. The arcade carried the gabled roofs of both the aisle and the nave. Later, this new wall line proved ill-founded and had to be buttressed, as can be seen on an engraving of the church made in 1733 (**74**). Wall paintings still surviving inside the east end of the new south aisle show that the Lady Chapel was located here. The status of the church also changed at this time, the existing college of three canons being replaced after 1347 by a vicar appointed by the Abbot of Haughmond.

The 1350 tenants' rental provides us with the first known names of the ordinary villagers, notable among whom is *Johannes at Walle* whose name may be derived from the fact that he farmed close by the ruins of the public baths which since the sixteenth century at least have been known as the 'Old Works'. Alternatively, he may have farmed the fields close by the city ramparts which although denuded would still have formed a formidable barrier to agriculture. There is some evidence too for the agricultural regime at Wroxeter and in its immediate hinterland in the form of the remains of strip cultivation, commonly known as ridge-and-furrow, which can still be seen in surviving earthworks near the Wroxeter Hotel, but which have also been traced in aerial photographs and geophysical survey. This method of cultivation is likely to have persisted into the eighteenth century but was established much earlier and its remains show that the bulk of the area enclosed within the ramparts had developed a soil sufficient to support agriculture by the later middle ages. It may be then that the

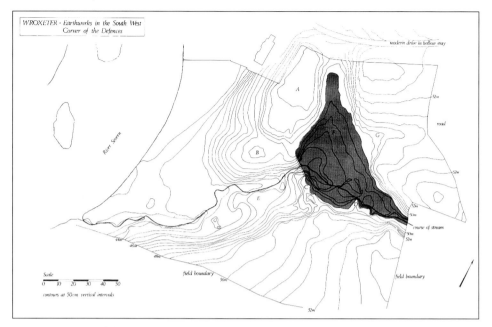

73 *A contour map of the earthworks in the field south-west of Wroxeter church. The site of the former mill pond is shown in darker tone. The manor house may have occupied the platform, A*

frigidarium, whose north wall still stands as the Old Work, was used as a barn, as was suggested by the burnt grain found on its floor in 1859. A pointer to a medieval date is provided by the complete late-medieval pipkin found in the ruins of one of the heated rooms in the mid-1930s. It may be that in addition to using the *frigidarium* as a granary, other parts of the baths buildings were being used at this late date. The fact that the walls of the baths are preserved to a greater height than any other Roman building in the city shows that they had, for some reason, not been robbed out in earlier times and may have been re-roofed for occupation, even if only as outbuildings. As a result, the area did not develop a soil deep enough for cultivation.

Although the other buildings of the city had largely been levelled and buried, and the area within the defences been transformed into fields, one other element of the city survived in addition to the ramparts and the ruins of the baths: its roads. The proof that some of Wroxeter's roads survived in use right through the period is of course that some are still used today. Among them are the main north–south street, Roman Watling Street, and Patch Lane, which runs along the line of the south side of the fortress. Another survival is the continuation of the street on the northern side of the baths *insula*. This stayed in use as a green lane until the mid-1970s and its continuation beyond the city walls can be traced in tracks, holloways and hedge-lines as far as Little Wenlock at the foot of the Wrekin. Also visible as a farm track for several miles is the important south-western branch of Watling Street towards the Craven Arms gap, which was used during the early modern period as a haulage road for coal brought by barge to a wharf on the Severn opposite Wroxeter church (**75**). These roads became more like green lanes than roads but their continued use is clear nonetheless.

74 *The south side of Wroxeter church in 1733 showing the buttressing of the late medieval south aisle wall*

After the mid-fourteenth century, the population seems to have remained relatively static and there is certainly little evidence that a collapse was brought about by the Black Death in the latter half of that century. The richly humic soil caused by the decay of Wroxeter's Roman buildings and the rubbish left by the city's inhabitants ensured the fertility of the land in comparison with the much lighter, sandier soils beyond the walls. That the village continued to flourish is shown once again in the fabric of the church both by the magnificent fourteenth-century iron-bound parish chest still there and by the erection of its impressive tower at the west end in the fifteenth century, with a later storey being added in the sixteenth century. This upper part of the church tower was further embellished with elaborate carved stonework in the distinctive Grinshill sandstone, a stone not otherwise seen at Wroxeter since the quarry was not exploited by the Romans. This sculpture, including the figures of SS Peter and Paul, is probably derived from Haughmond Abbey whose dissolution took place in 1539. This must have been a time of great change within the church itself with the medieval wall paintings, fragments of which were uncovered briefly in the restoration work of 1986, being whitewashed to be replaced by plain religious texts and the arms of the crown. The rood screen and medieval fittings of the church were taken away and burnt so that the once richly gaudy interior became the plain, white interior with box-pews familiar today. With the change in the religious order came new families who supported the new faith and the Tudor dynasty. At Wroxeter they are represented by the Newports whose tombs dominate the east end of the church. They may have been responsible for funding the work on the tower and for the remodelling of the east window into a single perpendicular five-light structure to replace the Norman five-light window.

75 *A view of Watling Street South at Brompton with Wroxeter church tower in the distance. The road must have looked much like this throughout the Middle Ages*

From the sixteenth century onward there seems to have been a gradual decline in Wroxeter's wealth and importance. The most obvious sign of this was the 1763 rebuilding of the south aisle wall which had begun to collapse through poor foundations and lack of maintenance. The new wall was positioned half way between the medieval wall and the Anglo-Saxon one, reflecting the overall decline in population, the new work needing only a single roof over the nave and aisle, and the conversion of the former Lady Chapel into a vestry. With these additions and changes the church reached the form in which it now survives today, the only major modern addition being a porch built in the 1890s.

Despite the smaller population, however, some of the villagers were people of some wealth, as is shown by the four substantial seventeenth-century timber-framed cottages still surviving and the imposing former vicarage next to the church whose core is of a similar date. The peak of settlement, recorded as 112 houses in the 1812 census, is shown on the 1840 tithe map which records the dense medieval landscape of Wroxeter just before its decline. This occurred between 1840–80, a remarkably short time in which the densely-occupied core of the village between the river and the church was reduced to a single croft, Topsy Cottage. A few other houses also survived around the church and a row of mid-nineteenth-century labourers' cottages perhaps represents improved living conditions for some of the villagers but the larger part of the population seems to have melted away with the coming of modern transport, and especially the railway, perhaps to live in Shrewsbury. This sudden emigration may well have been caused by the increasing mechanisation of agriculture forcing the inhabitants to seek work elsewhere. Whatever the precise causes, the village dwindled to a few cottages around the church, and has only revived in this century with the building of an hotel, and a row of modern council houses and other cottages outside the defences to the south.

Visitors to the site today can visit the church and see the village, but access to the Roman city is currently limited to the remains on the baths *insula* and the forum colonnade on the other side of the Watling Street. As yet there is nothing to disturb the tranquillity of the site, and there is certainly little sign of archaeological work. There seems little doubt that Wroxeter's importance as one of the last great unexplored Romano-British urban sites will ensure its continued survival, but equally the inevitable desire to preserve should not be allowed to bring the total cessation of active archaeological work on the site. Archaeologists will continue to need training; new techniques will need to be field-tested and where better could one achieve such ends? On the academic level too, a strong case can be made for further work. The Wroxeter Hinterland Project, and in particular the geophysical plan of the city, has certainly added considerably to our understanding of the site, though no one would argue that it has told us all that there is to know about Wroxeter. Much still remains to be done, particularly in examining the earliest and latest phases of the site, and in discovering how people actually made their living within the city. Unless this process of interrogation and analysis of information is allowed to proceed with the addition of fresh discoveries, the site is liable to become fossilised without being able to achieve fully its potential of answering some of the most fundamental questions relating to Romano-British life.

Further reading

General

There are a great many books on Roman Britain. The standard works remain Sheppard Frere's *Britannia* (3rd edn 1987) and Peter Salway's *Roman Britain* (1981). Both books take a generally historical, and often Roman-centred, view of the subject. In contrast, Martin Millett's *The Romanization of Roman Britain* (1990) takes a more archaeologically-orientated approach. Non-specialists might find his book *Roman Britain* (1995) more approachable, however. For the later period, Simon Esmonde Cleary's *The Ending of Roman Britain* (1989) provides much useful information on how Roman Britain was affected by the changes in the later Roman empire. *An Atlas of Roman Britain* (1990) by Barri Jones and David Mattingly gives a good visual summary of the development of Roman Britain.

There are many books on various themes which will help to put Wroxeter and its hinterland into context. A good introduction to Roman forts and their organisation in Britain and Germany is Anne Johnson's *Roman Forts* (1983). For the Roman army, an excellent overview is provided by Graham Webster's *The Roman Imperial Army* (3rd edn 1985). On towns, John Wacher's *Towns in Roman Britain* (2nd edn 1995) and Barry Burnham and John Wacher's *Small Towns of Roman Britain* (1990) provide detailed case studies of the principal settlements. The first of these includes a good summary of the previous excavations at Wroxeter. For a more general introduction to town and countryside in the Roman period, Guy de la Bédoyère's *Roman Towns in Britain* (1992) and *Roman Villas and the Countryside* (1993) can be recommended. The latter topic can also be followed up in Richard Hingley's *Rural Settlement in Roman Britain* (1989) and Ken and Petra Dark's *The Landscape of Roman Britain* (1997). Martin Henig's books on *Art in Roman Britain* (1995) and *Religion in Roman Britain* (1984) provide good guides to these subjects and feature material from Wroxeter. Ann Woodward's *Shrines and Sacrifice* (1992) deals with the archaeology of Romano-British religion and examines the transition to Christianity. The classic guide to this latter aspect, however, is still Charles Thomas' *Christianity in Roman Britain to AD 500* (1981).

Wroxeter and the *Cornovii*

Books on the excavations within the city include Thomas Wright's *Uriconium* (1872) and J.P. Bushe-Fox's *Excavations on the site of the Roman Town at Wroxeter, in 1912* (1913). The second and third volumes, covering the 1913 and 1914 seasons, had virtually identical titles and were published respectively in 1914 and 1916. These three reports were produced as volumes 1, 2 and 4 of the Society of Antiquaries of London Research Report series. Donald Atkinson's report on the forum was produced by the Birmingham and Warwickshire Archaeological Society as *Report on Excavations at Wroxeter (the Roman city of* Viroconium*) in the county of Salop, 1923–7*. It can be found in the original (wartime) edition (1942) or the better-quality 1970 reprint. All of these may still occasionally be available in second-hand bookshops. More minor excavation reports are scattered in a number of articles in various journals, the references to which are mostly to be found in *The Cornovii*, mentioned below.

Of the modern excavations only one is currently in print, although two others are in production and another has been commissioned. That in print is *The Baths Basilica, Wroxeter. Excavations 1966–90* (1997) by Philip Barker, Roger White, Kate Pretty, Heather Bird and Mike Corbishley (available from English Heritage). The two volumes in production relate to the military phase of Wroxeter and to the evidence for the baths and *macellum*. These too will be English Heritage publications. The last report will appear as a future volume of the transactions of the Shropshire Archaeological and Historical Society and will cover the many minor excavations carried out in the last 30 years.

Work on the Wroxeter Hinterland Project is still in progress but interim reports will soon be available in major journals. In the meantime, details are also available on the World Wide Web at **http://www.bufau.ac.uk./**. The virtual reality reconstructions of the city and fortress, funded by BT, will be available on the www site, or as a CD-ROM from 1999.

The principal work on the tribe remains *The Cornovii* by Graham Webster (2nd edn 1991). The same author's book *Rome against Caratacus* (2nd edn 1993) provides a useful summary of the evidence for the Roman conquest of Cornovian territory. For a general archaeological survey of the area, Stan Stanford's *Archaeology of the Welsh Marches* (2nd edn 1991) is a good introduction. These books can be usefully supplemented by the excellent photographs and text in *Shropshire from the Air* (1993) by Mike Watson and Chris Musson. A useful collection on aspects of the archaeology of Wroxeter and its landscape is *From Roman Viroconium to Medieval Wroxeter* (1990), edited by Philip Barker.

For the early medieval background, Margaret Gelling's general work *The West Midlands in the Early Middle Ages* (1992) is the best current guide. A slightly different view of the evidence is taken by Nick Higham in *The Origins of Cheshire* (1993). A good general history of the Anglo-Saxon conquest is provided in Barbara Yorke's *Kings and Kingdoms of Early Anglo-Saxon England* (1990). *Civitas to Kingdom* by Ken Dark (1994) gives an overview of the emergence of the early Celtic kingdoms in the west. Some of his views are highly speculative but are intriguing nonetheless. The same might also be said of John Morris' *The Age of Arthur* (1975) which looks at the emergence of both the British and Anglo-Saxon kingdoms of Britain. The early Welsh poems, which are linguistically particularly difficult to translate, are available in a number of versions of which the most recent, *Early Welsh Saga Poetry* by Jenny Rowlands (1990), is the best. It provides a text and translation with extensive footnotes and discussion.

Techniques

For an excellent description of the basic geophysical techniques, Tony Clark's *Seeing beneath the soil* is highly recommended (1990). Place-name studies can be followed up in Margaret Gelling's work *Signposts to the Past* (1978). The techniques and pitfalls of aerial photography are outlined in *Air photo interpretation for archaeologists* by David Wilson (1982).

The books written by Philip Barker on archaeological techniques, namely *Techniques of Archaeological Excavation* (1st edn 1977, 2nd edn 1982, 3rd edn 1993; each edition is extensively revised), and *Understanding Archaeological Excavation* (1986), rely for many of their examples on the excavations at Wroxeter and detail some of the discoveries made there. For a more general guide, Kevin Greene's *Introduction to Archaeology* (3rd edn 1995) is a useful book.

Glossary

automated resistivity meter A geophysical instrument which can take and log resistivity readings continuously whilst being pulled across the ground (see resistivity).

axonometric A form of projection used to reconstruct buildings by drawing vertical lines directly from a plan. In this way, the absolute dimensions are kept to scale.

baths basilica In Latin, *basilica thermarum*. A hall or large room attached to the main rooms of a bath house where one could exercise, or merely socialise, before taking a bath. Such rooms or halls became increasingly important in bath houses, even where the climate was suitable for exercising outside all the year round.

caldarium A directly-heated room in a bath house with a humid atmosphere provided by the hot plunge bath above the furnace. A Turkish bath is a modern equivalent.

canabae Literally, 'the booths'. An area, immediately adjacent to a fort and under military control, where civilians lived and worked. Taverns, brothels and perhaps workshops were located here where the garrison might spend their spare time (see *vicus*).

congregational church An early Christian church provided within the city walls for services. Burials would still have taken place outside the city walls.

constitutio Antoniniana A law, promulgated in 212 by the Emperor Caracalla (whose official name was Marcus Antoninus), which made all free-born people in the empire Roman citizens.

cornucopia A 'horn of plenty', usually shown overflowing with fruit, held by a god or goddess. A symbol of fruitfulness and abundance.

cullet Broken glass collected for recycling by glassworkers.

154

cupellation	A smelting technique to extract silver or gold from lead and other base metals by melting lead in a furnace over bone ash. The introduction of oxygen causes the lead to combine with the ash, leaving the silver behind. The ash is then resmelted to extract the lead.
forum	An open square used for a market. In Britain, the square was usually surrounded on three sides by colonnades with shops. The fourth side had a basilican hall where the town council met and local courts were held.
forum boarium	Literally a 'cattle market'. A market place for the buying and selling of all livestock. Generally in a different location from the forum proper.
frigidarium	A room in a bath house without any heating other than free-standing braziers or other such arrangements. Usually the first room in a bath house, it may also act as an undressing room.
glacis	A bank sloping down from a rampart on which attackers would be exposed to defender's missiles.
gradiometry meter	a geophysical instrument which measures minute variations in the earth's magnetic field caused by human or geological disturbances.
ground penetrating radar	A geophysical technique which sends microwave pulses into the ground and records the varying signal reflected back by buried remains. The signals are recorded as vertical slices which can then be combined and resliced horizontally by computer software to produce plans at different depths (see **37**).
hypocaust	A system of underfloor heating.
isometric	A technique used to reconstruct buildings by drawing vertical lines directly from a plan whose opposing angles have been altered. The resulting drawing gives a perspective view of the structure.
labarum	A late Roman battle standard consisting of a shaft carrying a square flag surmounted by the *chi-rho*, Christ's initials in Greek.
macellum	A specialised market hall consisting of several shops, generally arranged around a courtyard, where high-class meat and game could be purchased.
mansio	An inn or hostel provided for travelling officials at regular intervals along the road network, and within cities and small towns.
martyrium	An early Christian church built over the tomb of a martyr (presumed or actual). Generally, these were

located outside the city walls as burials were not permitted within the walled area.

mortarium
A mixing bowl with a gritted interior used with a pestle to grind food. A specialist vessel produced in various centres which may carry the name of the potter stamped on the rim.

natatio
A shallow outdoor pool in a bath complex used by bathers to cool themselves down after they had been in the hot rooms.

palaestra
The outdoor exercise area provided for bathers in a public baths.

plumbata (pl. *plumbatae*)
A late Roman dart with a long, lead-weighted shank. Used as an anti-personnel weapon.

resistivity
A geophysical technique which passes a small electrical current through the ground and measures the resistance to that current caused by buried features (see automated resistivity).

robber trench
A trench dug to extract stone from a ruined building or its foundations.

rubble platform
A level area of rubble, often packed with mortar, plaster or earth, laid to form a foundation for a timber-framed building.

samian ware
A type of pottery made in northern Italy, southern, central, and eastern Gaul, and in other minor centres. A glossy red-slipped ware, in plain or relief decorated forms, which was mass-produced in the first century BC until the collapse of the industry in the mid-third century.

stylobate
Large blocks of stone used as the foundation of a colonnade.

sudatorium
A directly-heated room in a bath house with a dry atmosphere. A modern equivalent is a sauna.

tepidarium
The room separating unheated and heated rooms in a bath house. Its function was to act as a heat lock so that heat did not escape from the main hot rooms.

thegn
An Anglo-Saxon aristocrat.

timber-framing
A method of construction using large timbers held together by mortise and tenon joints to create frames. These form a free-standing structure which has no need of foundations.

vicus
A term used for the civilian settlement close by a fort. Such a settlement might contain the *mansio* (q.v.), temples, and shops alongside the houses of locals (see *canabae*).

Index